THE NEWS MEDIA
What Makes Them Tick?

John L. Hulteng

Stanford University

Prentice-Hall, Inc., Englewood Cliffs, New Jersey 07632

Library of Congress Cataloging in Publication Data

HULTENG, JOHN L.   (date)
    The news media.

    (Perspectives in mass communication)
    Bibliography: p.
    Includes index.
    1. Journalism. I. Title. II. Series.
PN4731.H82   070.4   78–15233
    ISBN 0–13–621086–4

PRENTICE-HALL PERSPECTIVES IN MASS COMMUNICATION SERIES
edited by John L. Hulteng and Edward J. Trayes

© 1979 by Prentice-Hall, Inc., Englewood Cliffs, New Jersey 07632

Printed in the United States of America

10 9 8 7 6 5 4 3 2

Editorial/production supervision and interior design by Lynda Heideman
Cover design by Hernandez-Porto
Manufacturing buyer: Trudy Pisciotti

PRENTICE-HALL INTERNATIONAL, INC., *London*

PRENTICE-HALL OF AUSTRALIA PTY. LIMITED, *Sydney*

PRENTICE-HALL OF CANADA, LTD., *Toronto*

PRENTICE-HALL OF INDIA PRIVATE LIMITED, *New Delhi*

PRENTICE-HALL OF JAPAN, INC., *Tokyo*

PRENTICE-HALL OF SOUTHEAST ASIA PTE. LTD., *Singapore*

WHITEHALL BOOKS LIMITED, *Wellington, New Zealand*

For Roy Paul Nelson

Contents

Series Editors' Note

The Perspectives in Mass Communication series offers great flexibility to instructors and students in courses in communication or the mass media and society area. Each volume in the series deals with a specific aspect of mass communication, and each is authored by scholars chosen for their competence to develop that topic intensively and authoritatively.

Among the volumes included in this series is one that inventories the media fields today and traces historical and developmental patterns. Another identifies and analyzes the forces and motivations that influence the functioning of contemporary news media. One volume views the media as expressions of popular culture and examines their significance in that role. Others explore a range of relevant topics, including the theories of mass communication and the interrelationship between the advertising industry and the media.

This modular approach allows for combining two, three, or more of the compact volumes in the series into a composite text, permitting the instructor to tailor the text materials to the emphases desired in a particular course or to the needs of a particular group of students. An individual title may also be used as the core text for an introductory course on its topic.

Taken as a whole, the series provides a comprehensive, multi-dimensional understanding of the media of mass communication, particularly those media devoted either primarily or in part to the dissemination of news, information, and opinion.

JOHN L. HULTENG
EDWARD J. TRAYES

SECTION ONE
THE MEDIA
AND
THE BOTTOM LINE

Robert Estabrook, for 25 years an editorial writer and foreign correspondent for the *Washington Post,* left that paper in 1971 to follow out the dream of many newsmen and newswomen—he bought a small country newspaper and became his own boss, editor and publisher of the *Lakeville* (Connecticut) *Journal* (circulation 5571).

Five years later he was asked by his former colleagues to answer the question: how do you feel about the switch?

In response Estabrook cited the 60- to 80-hour work weeks, the night meetings to cover, the angry subscribers to mollify. And then he said: "Would we give it up? Of course not." He and his wife, it appeared, truly loved the roles they had taken on.

Expanding upon his answer, Estabrook offered this warning to any of his friends who might also be considering venturing into ownership: "Country journalism must be a business before it can be a profession. Long before you can register editorial excellence you need to apply business expertise."[1]

Estabrook was noting a home truth that applies to all journalistic ventures, from his *Lakeville Journal* to the *Los Angeles Times*, from the small-market radio station in Ontario, Oregon, to the CBS Television Network, from the *Western Stamp Collector* to *Newsweek.*

To get a chance to perform whatever functions they want to perform in society, mass media enterprises must first establish themselves as viable business ventures, able to stay afloat economically. They must some-how generate from various sources sufficient income so that the publishers, station managers, or magazine publishers can do their thing, whatever it may be.

1
A *Sine Qua Non*

Some critics of the media, and members of the public who lack experience with the workings of the media, often overlook two fundamental facts about mass communication ventures in any medium:

1. they are basically business enterprises;
2. but they differ from most other business enterprises in the all-important respect that making money often is *not* their chief reason for being.

A car manufacturer or a pickle producer wants to turn out a product that will beat the competition and attract a maximum number of buyers. In each case, the aim is to come out ahead financially at the close of the year. A maximum return to the owner or to the stockholders is the chief objective of management in either case.

Some news media businesses may not differ much from the car maker or the pickle factory. It is not difficult to single out newspapers, radio stations, TV stations, or magazines that are obviously run primarily to produce the fattest possible profits. The first Lord Thomson of Fleet, who built one of the largest worldwide journalistic empires, freely admitted that he acquired newspapers because they made money for him ("I'd be a fool otherwise, wouldn't I?").

But a great many media owners and operators see their properties in a different light. It is necessary, to be sure, that the newspaper or station or magazine show a profit; otherwise it would go out of business altogether. But for those owners and managers with the broader perception, making a profit and thus staying afloat is a means to an end, not an end in itself. They see their media enterprises not only as economic ventures but as public service agencies with a vital, even indispensable role in the functioning of our representative system of government: providing the public with an understandable, comprehensive picture of the social and political systems in which we must somehow interact, make decisions and accommodations, survive—and maybe even be happy.

For the great majority of news media people who recognize the dual nature of the enterprises for which they work, life can be complicated by tensions, pressures, and relationships. How should they balance the urgent economic realities against the public service obligation? How can they reconcile the need for journalism ''to be a business before it can be a profession'' with the equally felt need to bring to the public as quickly as possible news that must be known and acted upon before it is too late? How can they produce a news product enticing enough to attract readers, hearers, or viewers, yet also solid enough to provide those consumers with the information they must have to function intelligently as citizens in a free society?

Let's begin this exploration of how the news media tick by looking at some of the relationships inherent in the dual roles of these media. What ties exist between news media and the sources of revenue upon which the media depend for survival: advertisers, subscribers, financial ''angels''? How tightly do those ties bind the public service aspirations of editors, reporters, or commentators?

How does ownership or ownership management relate to the ''working press,'' the women and men covering and reporting the news, aiming the cameras, editing the copy? How free, at various levels, are rank-and-file staff members to do their jobs as they perceive them? To what degree are they constrained by the philosophy or economic needs of ownership? This is the first focus of this book.

It is essential, however, to enter a *caveat* here.

Because we are beginning this overall survey of how the media tick by looking at bottom-line considerations, the reader may wrongly assume that in the author's eyes these considerations are paramount. That isn't the case.

As has been noted, *most* news media people do sense (though not always in the same ways) that the ultimate justification for their work is a public adequately and accurately informed about the world. As James Reston, the *New York Times* columnist, once put it:

> The events that are most important to the lives of our readers . . . are often very complicated and boring, and while a newspaper can easily go broke by reporting what's significant rather than what's personal or spicy, this is the primary responsibility of a serious newspaper.[2]

We are beginning with a look at the media and the bottom line not because the bottom line is *the* most important, but because it constitutes a *sine qua non*. Without economic independence, no media enterprise can continue to exist and perform its other functions.

It is probably necessary to acknowledge again that for *some* news media owners, managers, and workers, the bottom line is everything. But not for most. That is an essential point to bear in mind as we move on.

2
Media
and Advertisers

The web of relationships between the media and the advertisers whose dollars keep those media going varies from medium to medium. It varies, too, according to the size of the media outlet being examined. In all cases, however, the relationships grow out of a condition basic to all business interchange.

Any buyer-seller combination is interdependent. In some situations, the advantage lies with the buyer. A car dealer nearing the end of a model year may be overstocked; a buyer knowing this can talk the price down. Or the edge may lie with the seller: a gasoline crunch puts compact, gas-saving cars at a premium and dealers can pad their prices.

The size of the purchase involved can play a part, as well. An individual pays one price when he trades in his old car on a new model; a fleet buyer for a large firm pays a much lower unit rate for exactly the same sort of car the individual bought; bulk purchasing gives the fleet buyer considerable bargaining leverage.

Similar considerations hold in the relationships between advertisers and the news media. The newspapers and broadcast outlets have space or air time to sell. For a price they offer access to potential buyers held temporarily captive by their interest in the entertainment segments spaced between the TV commercials, or in the newspaper's news columns located strategically close to the ads.

A struggling radio station in a competitive market may offer bargain-priced spots to the advertiser; an entrenched monopoly newspaper may need the advertiser less than the advertiser needs the newspaper's access to the public, so its ad rates may not be subject to negotiation. In the former case, the advantage lies with the advertiser; in the latter, with the news medium.

The bulk purchase effect is evident in the media fields, too. The advertiser who regularly buys many pages of space in a magazine or newspaper pays a lower rate per line of type or column inch of space than does the one-shot advertiser. Radio and television rate cards show comparable variations.

The media-advertiser relationships that we have been discussing are straightforward counterparts of the relationships that exist in virtually all buyer-seller situations. But there is a crucial difference between buyer-seller relationships in the media and those same relationships in almost all other business transactions.

In most such transactions, the application of relative clout, the bargaining, the exploitation of timing, all focus on one thing: the price to be paid for the good or service under consideration. There may be subtleties involved— corporate favors to important clients, kickbacks to purchasing agents, bribes to foreign officials—but it all comes down to the central question of the final price to be paid, in cash or kind.

In the bargaining relationship between media seller and advertiser buyer, however, something else may be on the block as well as price: influence over the news, information, or entertainment content of the medium involved.

For the media of mass communication (most of them, anyway) do not exist solely as purveyors of advertising time on the air or of newspaper or magazine space. They also are the channels through which the public draws virtually all of the information it gets about the events, issues, and personalities of our time. It is enormously tempting to an advertiser with clout to make a try, at least, at parlaying a business transaction into something more than that; to try to use the media-advertiser relationship to alter, perhaps ever so slightly, the flow of information to the public.

The advertiser who buys billboard space, or relies on direct mail (bargain offers, coupons, fliers, all distributed by third class mail), has no chance to attempt to exploit the extra-dimension opportunity to influence mass media content. He is making a pitch on his own, gaining your attention or getting into your mailbox without the help of a news medium as carrier or introducer. The same thing is true to a considerable extent of the advertiser who relies on a ''shopper,'' a throw-away sheet delivered free to every doorstep, containing almost nothing but advertising, with perhaps a smattering of canned news or some bland snippets of local bulletin board information.

But an advertiser who buys a one-minute spot on the local radio station or a quarter-page ad in the local newspaper comes to you, in effect, introduced by the station or the paper. He enters your home in the company of a familiar voice, or a welcomed source of news. This is an obvious advantage to the advertiser; the entrée is what he pays for. That is a clear-cut transaction.

Sometimes, however, as a condition for purchasing those radio spots or that newspaper space, the advertiser tries to get a bonus. He tries to use the fact that he is an important economic mainstay for the station or newspaper as a basis for requesting that the medium put a special ''puff'' item on the air or in the paper (in essence, free advertising). Or he may propose that an embarrassing news break be suppressed for a crucial day or two. At this point the media-advertiser relationship has taken an ugly turn, one in which the public has an immediate and urgent interest. This is the point at which the media-advertiser relationship becomes significantly different from most other buyer-seller relationships.

The questions then arise: how often does this sort of pressure play take place? Under what conditions does the maneuver get results, from the advertiser's viewpoint? What are the consequences for the public?

At this juncture a couple of points deserve to be underlined.

Up to now we have cast the advertiser as the villain of the piece, seeking to take advantage of the media and tamper with news and entertainment content. In fairness, it should be noted that not all such situations are cases of rape. Sometimes the medium involved gives its willing consent and may even initiate the compromising circumstance.

Second, we should observe that up to this point we have been sketching the media-advertiser relationship in broad terms, as though the numerous media were uniform, monolithic. They aren't, of course, and the degree to which advertisers seek and sometimes obtain influence over the nonadvertising content of the media varies widely among those various media, and among different enterprises within a single medium. Let's explore some of the differences and see why there are differences.

A SPECTRUM OF DEPENDENCE

One basis for the differences is degree of dependence on advertising revenue. Newspapers obtain 55 to 70 percent of their total income from advertising; most of the remainder comes from sales of newspapers to subscribers or newsstand buyers.

Magazines get 45 to 60 percent of their total income from advertising, the remainder from circulation.

Radio and television, by contrast, are totally dependent on advertising revenue, except for a few public subscription stations or those underwritten by a rich angel (someone who can afford to support a money-losing venture, as a gesture of public service or perhaps to further a cause).

On the basis of these bald statistics, it would seem that the broadcast media would be the most vulnerable to advertiser influence, the magazines least vulnerable, and newspapers somewhere in between. But it's not not quite that simple. Each of the media must be considered separately, since each of them represents a special case with individual complexities and modifications.

Let's look first at newspapers. Here, size and the presence or absence of competition are factors that influence greatly a given publication's vulnerability to advertiser influence.

The smalltown weekly newspaper publisher could be badly hurt if a couple of the largest local advertisers pulled their lineage in pique over an editorial stand, or over an investigative news story an energetic reporter had uncovered. The loss of two major advertisers might spell the difference between survival and bankruptcy, since profit margins for very small newspapers are fragile.

A 250,000-circulation metropolitan daily with no competition might scarcely notice or care if even a big space buyer canceled his advertising; with no comparable channel in town (the electronic media do compete with the print media for a given advertiser's budget, but the type of advertising access to consumers offered differs widely between them, so the competition is not on a plane), the monopoly metro could count on the advertiser's coming back sooner or later, hat in one hand and advertising budget in the other. Or, if that particular advertiser didn't return, replacements could be found. This scenario has been played out many times. (In Portland, Oregon, a major department store pulled its advertising from the *Oregonian* because that paper had reported an instance of labor unrest at the store—and in a few months meekly asked to be let back in. In another case, this one in New York, a major automobile manufacturer withdrew all advertising from the *Wall Street Journal* after that paper printed a scoop on the manufacturer's next year's design, without causing even momentary distress to the *Journal*'s business manager.)

Most American cities that have daily newspapers have only one paper, or at the most a morning-evening combination managed by a single ownership. (In only about 3 percent of the cities with dailies is there any genuine newspaper competition; and in recent years virtually every attempt to launch a competitive paper where a well-established daily already was being published has failed.) Thus it would appear that insofar as daily newspapers are concerned, the specter of advertising pressure could fairly easily be exorcised or ignored.

Many weekly newspapers are members of groups or chains, and through the group association they gain an independence of advertisers comparable to that of the dailies. But individually owned weekly publications are vastly more vulnerable to the introduction of competition in this era of inexpensive cold-type production methods and contract printing plants than are their bigger brothers, the dailies. For such small papers, advertiser pressure presumably should still constitute an ever-present reality to be reckoned with.

Both of the last-mentioned assumptions are subject to qualifications, however.

We have been outlining the *potential* for abuse, not the extent of such abuse. And whether the potential is realized may not depend only on the size of the newspaper entity under examination.

There are many mom-and-pop weeklies, for example, whose editors have firmly withstood intense advertiser pressure, even full-scale boycotts. Some have gone under; some have survived. The point is, the fact that a weekly operation is more vulnerable than a larger one doesn't mean that it will automatically knuckle under when an advertiser of importance throws some weight around.

At the other end of the scale, it is possible to cite instances of metropolitan newspaper giants that proved only too evidently amenable to advertiser influence, despite the theoretical insulation provided by their size. The *Denver Post,* for example, once provided many columns of trumped-up puff copy for a new shopping center, to win substantial legitimate advertising from the center. More recently, when Sears, Roebuck, one of Chicago's merchandising giants, was charged by the Federal Trade Commission with bait and switch violations, most of the great Chicago-based media somehow decided the story wasn't newsworthy. They gave it no coverage at all in some cases, and only passing mention in others. To obtain this convenient blackout, Sears apparently didn't even have to flex any of its advertising budget muscle—the papers took it upon themselves not to offend one of their best customers.[3]

The Sears case suggests one other point about advertiser influence on the nonadvertising content of newspapers.

The blatant power play by an advertiser bent on getting free space or on blacking out awkward news may in fact be rare in today's newspaper world, particularly with respect to the metropolitan press armored by monopolistic or semimonopolistic status. Such approaches are not so rare, unhappily, in small communities where less insulated publishers must walk warily in the presence of major advertisers.

Yet power is not the only means by which advertiser influence over news content may be exerted. There are subtler ploys.

In the Sears-FTC case, there is no indication that an executive of the big firm made the media rounds, demanding that the story be buried. Somehow the media managers who controlled the news spigots in Chicago knew intuitively that they would be better off not to touch this one.

How many times this sort of half-aware backstage editing of the news takes place on big newspapers and small only the editors and copy desk chiefs know in their hearts. It happens at least some of the time, certainly, and without a glove being laid on an editor by a pugnacious advertiser. An unspoken understanding seeps around the newsroom; it becomes a ''given'' that the news not contain details that would give egregious offense to the advertisers whose dollars underwrite much of the cost of publication. So the make of a car involved in a fatal crash is not mentioned; the driver was in ''a late-model compact.'' If a guest jumps to her death from a tenth floor hotel window, it won't show up in print that she was staying at the Plaza. It will be "a west-side hotel." (But persons who commit suicide from the Golden Gate Bridge are never described as having "leaped from a downtown bridge.")

It is very easy, even painless, for those who process news copy to make these minor concessions to the sensitivity of advertisers. So great a volume of news comes in to the average city desk that inevitably a substantial fraction finds its way to the spike or to the wastebasket. James Reston of the *New York Times* notes that "on the *New York Times* we put 2,000,000 words a day through our hands and we print 100,000. We struggle and differ over what those 100,000 should be." [4]

At the *Times* we can feel confident that that struggle is an earnest and fearless one. If there are sacred cows in the *Times* city room, it is pretty certain that they aren't advertisers.

But what about the same sort of struggle (likely on a smaller scale) in the city rooms in Indianapolis, Indiana, or Petaluma, California—or Chicago? The incidence of tacit accommodation to advertiser interest in the news column content of newspapers—even when that accommodation isn't overtly pursued—is beyond our capacity to know or estimate. Nonetheless, it *is* a factor, and more to be concerned about, perhaps, than the open pressure play.

There are other ways in which advertisers or other special interests may find it possible to mold the news content of newspapers.

Columbia Journalism Review, perhaps the most demanding and consistent monitor of press performance in our day, recently noted (not for the first time) how frequently newspapers will swallow whole and pass on as straight news the press releases ground out daily by businesses, government, and other institutions.

What attracted *CJR*'s attention this time was a press release from Boeing Corporation, and the almost verbatim use of that release in the *Seattle Times*. The release was carefully constructed to emphasize some good news about Boeing in the lead paragraphs (sales and earnings for the company were up) and to bury in the second half of the release the bad news (employment was down by 5700 jobs).

Of course, there is nothing inherently wrong about a newspaper making use of a press release as the basis for a news item. Many press releases are straightforward, factual reports; they provide a news source that newspapers and other media must depend on for access to certain types of news that may not be important enough to warrant staff coverage.

But good reporters and discriminating editors know that press releases cannot always be accepted uncritically, touched up a bit, fitted with a headline, and sent on to be processed into the paper or onto the newscast. Many press releases have an axe to grind, or a special twist to put on the news—usually to the benefit of the company putting out the release. As the *Columbia Journalism Review* editors observed:

It's no secret that Seattle is a company town, and that Boeing is the company. . . . And Boeing's own version of what was news in the Seattle area, rather than a reporter's, was printed in *The Seattle Times* without its readers knowing it.[5]

It may be time to step back a bit and see how we've come out to this point. Generalizations are always risky, and doubly so in the case of the news media. But it is fair to say that our exploration of the relationships between advertisers and the newspaper segment of the press has left us with at least a few defensible conclusions:

1. Advertiser pressure today is rarely applied directly in an effort to influence the nonadvertising content of newspapers.
2. This is particularly true with respect to the semimonopolistic large daily papers; the small community papers are more vulnerable, and that vulnerability is sometimes exploited.
3. Advertiser influence on news content may be exerted in less direct ways, and in the newsrooms of mighty metro giants as well as in the cramped office–composing room–editor's sanctum of the tiny country weekly.
4. The indirect infringement upon the integrity of the news may be of greater concern to us as consumers than the open power play, just because it *is* indirect, out of sight, and thus out of our ken.

To balance these conclusions, we might observe that while efforts are sometimes made to exploit the symbiotic advertiser-media relationship, this is by no means an everyday thing at most newspapers. As we suggested earlier, no one can really *know* how often the news flow is diverted or dammed up to benefit the interests of an important advertiser, either because pressure has been brought to bear or simply because a reporter or editor senses that this would be politic.

Even in the absence of statistics, it is possible to justify confidence in the basic integrity of the American newspaper press. I spent a dozen years working for newspapers in a variety of roles, from sports writer to editorial page editor, on weeklies, small-city dailies, and metropolitan monopolies. I've also spent more than 20 additional years closely observing the press from an academic vantage point. It is a personal conclusion, admittedly unsupported by hard evidence or incidence tables, that most newspaper people, most of the time, try to provide us with news that has not been distorted for or by any external influence, consciously or unconsciously. The journalistic ethic of providing an honest and comprehensive picture of the world is alive and well at most newspaper operations. This is, it should be repeated, a personal conclusion based on one individual's lifetime experience, and the reader may wish to discount it for that reason.

Now let's take a look at advertiser-media relationships in a different medium.

ADVERTISERS AND BROADCASTING

In the case of radio and television, media-advertiser relationships must be examined against a special historical backdrop.

Both of the electronic media grew up primarily as vehicles for the provision of entertainment to the public. The entertainment content was financed in one fashion or another by advertisers. Advertising revenue was the sole means of support for both radio and television, and still is today to a very substantial degree.

Just as it was necessary in the last section of this discussion to consider weekly newspapers and daily newspapers separately, as somewhat different animals though of the same species, so it is necessary now to consider radio and television individually.

Radio grew to the status of a national industry largely on the basis of network programming; today it has become primarily a local medium. Television is the network medium of our era, with its local aspects subordinate.

This is a significant distinction, particularly when we are engaged in probing the relationships between media and advertisers. For network broadcasting developed through the years with the advertiser or his agent firmly in charge of the entertainment package that was the chief content element first of radio and later of television. The advertiser, or an advertising agency, put together the entertainment segment that would go on the air under the advertiser's sponsorship; the same source developed the commercial messages to accompany the entertainment. It was natural, under the circumstances, that the advertiser would want the content of the programs to be popular with the listening or viewing public *and* in harmony with the objectives of the advertiser's firm. In the early stages of network development, advertiser influence on the content of radio and television programs was strong and direct.

The situation today is somewhat altered, in that now the major television networks typically develop program packages and then invite advertisers to bid for the right to sponsor those programs and hitch to them their commercial messages. Advertiser influence has thus been diluted; but it hasn't been eliminated, by any means.

It is still possible, for example, for an automobile manufacturer to insist that the hero of a series sponsored by the manufacturer always be shown driving one of the sponsor's products.

It is still possible for a sponsor to request the deletion of a scene in an hour-long special, if that scene would reflect unfavorably upon the sponsor's firm, industry, or product. It is still possible (it happened in Philadelphia) for objections from a powerful advertiser to cause the dismissal of a commentator.

Perhaps most significant of all, it is still possible for advertisers to influence network content simply by refusing to sponsor controversial programs, or ones that might alienate a consumer segment. Unsponsored programs are a costly liability for the carrier and even the major networks can't afford to carry many of them. Thus, much network programming is safe, tested, lowest-common-denominator material, designed to offend few and to please as many as possible among the viewing public.

Maverick independent producers once in a while put together a show or a series on a touchy topic, build an audience by syndicating their show to non-network stations, and finally gain network acceptance. But they are exceptions to the general pattern of network television.

One highly pragmatic reason for the networks' preference for safe programming is money. Jeff Greenfield, a writer and political consultant who earlier worked for many years in advertising, points out that a single one-hour episode of a popular weekly TV series may cost the network as much as $300,000. An advertiser who wants to buy 30 seconds of time to make his pitch in the middle of that program may have to pay the network $60,000 for the slot, or $2,000 a second. And then the advertiser may invest as much as $200,000—more than $6,000 per second—in preparing with infinite care the commercial message that will occupy that fleeting segment of air time.[6] With such enormous sums at stake, the networks understandably don't want to take chances and the advertisers—equally understandably—are likely to want guarantees that the impact of their gold-plated commercials won't be offset by negative notes in program content.

The networks, the advertisers, and individual television stations all are acutely sensitive to the audience ratings earned by programs. Those ratings, compiled on the basis of diaries kept by test families, by telephone surveys, or by other methods—none of them infallible—are supposed to indicate what percentage of the available viewing public is watching a given program at a given hour.

The three major television networks, ABC, CBS, and NBC, compete tensely for the highest possible rating for their programming schedules. They array top-rated shows one after another, to hold a large audience over a long time span. Shows are juggled from one time slot to another to offset highly rated competition on another network, or to put together a combination that will capture the bulk of the viewing audience during the evening prime time.

This competition militates against the chancy program or the unproven formula, and in favor of the dependable mixture of situation comedies and vicarious violence that has been shown to be surefire through the years.

So, sometimes directly, sometimes indirectly through the economic nerve system of network television, the advertiser continues to affect significantly the content of the entertainment segment of network output.

What about news?

In the early days of radio, and later during the similar development phase of television, news was a minor factor in programming, almost an aside. But in recent years the television networks have discovered that news is as salable an ingredient in programming as the sit-coms and soap operas. Sponsors are eager to have their product messages associated with the major nightly news programs and their familiar avuncular or oracular anchor personages.

However, sponsors have not had and do not have the same degree of influence on the content of news programs as they are able to exert over entertainment segments.

It may be true that a network news producer might move commercials around on a given night's show, to avoid juxtaposing a sponsor's message with a news story reflecting unfavorably on that sponsor's industry. But that is usually as far as it goes. Advertisers do not try to exercise a veto power over individual news stories on the television networks, and wouldn't succeed if they did.

At the level of the local station there may be more sensitivity to the interests of advertisers, particularly in a highly competitive market situation. The local news program that typically precedes or follows the network offering may indeed be edited to avoid giving needless offense to local advertisers with big budgets to spend.

It should be noted, however, that most individual television stations with a network affiliation are affluent enough to afford independence, if their owners and managers truly want it. Affiliate stations get a part of their income from the networks, which pay them on a fixed basis for airing network programming; the networks are willing to pay because they need the affiliate audiences as a basis for attracting advertisers. So most of the programming offered on a local television station comes from the networks; the local station may develop only a few hours a day of local programming, chiefly news, talk shows, movies, and local sports events. This means that the local advertiser's clout with respect to the station is substantially diminished. The advertiser typically needs the station, and the access it provides to large local audiences, more than the station needs the individual advertiser. The network system leaves the local television station manager in a position to assert and maintain independence of advertiser influence—if this is what the manager wants.

Approximately 15 percent of the commercial television stations in the United States are independents—neither owned by nor affiliated with a network. They are far less secure financially, and at least some of them are more vulnerable to the pressures applied by local advertisers than are stations largely dependent on network-generated revenue. That doesn't mean, of course, that all of the independents succumb to such pressures; many are truly independent, in all senses of the word.

HOW ABOUT RADIO?

The network era in which we find American television today came a couple of decades earlier for radio. From the mid-1930s to the mid-1950s, radio was programmed by and dominated by the major networks as is now the case with television. But with the rapid penetration of TV in the 1950s, offering an entertainment package in two dimensions rather than radio's one, there was a swift and convulsive change in the nature of radio broadcasting.

At first many observers thought it was time to write radio's obituary; the industry's golden years were ended, and an empty future lay ahead. How could the disembodied voice of radio compete with the glowing tube and its live action?

In one sense the gloomy observers were right; radio could *not* compete with television on television's terms. But the obituaries were premature. Radio staggered but didn't fall. It found a niche of its own in the communication spectrum and settled down to stay.

Radio became a local and specialized medium. It capitalized on its ubiquity: radio can go anywhere with the listener—in the car, in the kitchen, in the woods, in the bathroom. TV is less mobile, at least for the time being.

The survival formula radio hit upon was a mixture of news, music, and sports, typically with a heavy emphasis on music. Rock music had become almost a new language for the young, and radio could deliver it to them anywhere. Country and western music drew yet another specialized audience segment. News could be packaged in staccato segments; commercials, of course, could be taped. A small-market radio station could be operated on a shoestring, by comparison with the costs involved in TV.

Radio today is thus relatively free of the kind of advertiser influence that is felt through the network system under which television operates, and under which the radio industry also operated in an earlier incarnation.

However, since it is a local medium, radio can be vulnerable to the pressure of local advertisers, particularly because radio remains a fiercely competitive medium. In a typical town there is usually only one daily newspaper; there may be one, two, or four TV stations, except in the very largest markets. But even in small communities there will be several radio stations, as many as a dozen in a town of 50,000 persons and up to 30 or more in a metropolitan center. Typically, too, only a few of them are truly prospering; most of the rest are scrambling to make ends meet, despite the low cost of the contemporary radio programming formula.

When competition is intense, a buyer's market prevails; the advertiser has greater leverage in the relationship between the medium and the advertiser.

But, as a practical matter, does the advertiser have much real reason to wield that leverage? If the station is geared to a top-40 formula (playing tapes of the 40 tunes that are currently most popular with the youthful listeners, over and over again through the broadcast day, interrupted only by the disc jockey's patter and the commercials), what is there for the advertiser to influence?

If news is part of the broadcast package, it is likely to be in terms of headlines for local items; national and international news usually comes in the form of a brief, hourly network summary, one of the few vestiges of the old network pattern that once was dominant. Few radio stations, except for some in the major population centers, can afford to mount a full-scale local news operation.

The annual Columbia-DuPont Survey of Broadcast Journalism, looking back over 1973 and 1974, noted that "radio was almost, but not quite, a journalistic desert."[7] Isolated examples of news enterprise were noted by the Columbia-DuPont analysts almost with wonder: ". . . this remarkable display of news energy and imagination was not likely to be repeated. . . ."[8]

So, while the local nature of radio and the intense competition in the field theoretically constitute fertile ground for the flowering of advertiser influence over the medium, there is neither reason nor occasion for this to happen with much frequency. At the most, perhaps, it could be assumed that the abbreviated local news reports would be sensitized to the pet peeves of important hometown advertisers and to the land mines hidden in touchy local controversies. Exactly how frequent are such concessions, an outside observer cannot know; so even the assumption should remain a qualified one.

(Lest a distorted impression be left by the "desert" assessment from the Columbia-DuPont survey, let it be noted that there are oases. Many classical music FM stations are in operation. So are a few all-news stations that try to provide more than headline snippets. And individual instances of genuine overall excellence can be singled out even in small communities.)

While advertisers may not infringe very often or very significantly on radio programming independence, another form of external influence—"plugola"—is distressingly prevalent among those stations appealing primarily to an audience segment attracted by a specific variety of music. The term refers to the practice of record producers and promoters offering various inducements, from free records to sums of money or supplies of drugs, to get their latest songs or their newest performers included on the station's current program list. Such plugola peddlers are not advertisers, of course, but their attempts to rig programming content must be included among the factors that make at least a part of the radio industry tick. Most station managers and disc jockeys, to their credit, resist such rigging efforts; but some of their brethren are more susceptible.

A SPECIAL CASE

Public radio and television broadcasting must be considered apart from the commercial industry. In theory at least, public broadcasting derives its chief financial support from tax revenue, channeled through federal, state, or regional agencies. There are no advertisers in the conventional sense. This arrangement is intended to give the producers and directors of public broadcasting a considerably freer hand than is enjoyed by their counterparts on the commercial stations and networks. They can tackle topics that would be considered too touchy for the networks, or devote time to other subjects or activities considered of much too limited interest to be marketed to commercial sponsors.

There are a couple of flaws in this theoretically happy picture, however: one inherent and one that developed in the late 1970s.

In public broadcasting there is an entity comparable to the sponsor or advertiser on commercial networks. Public funds flow to public broadcasters through government agencies that may have sensitivities as delicate as those of advertisers who buy time and programs in the commercial industry. And despite efforts to buffer public broadcasting from pressures exerted by government, those pressures can be and sometimes are felt.

During the Nixon era, for example, the administration tinkered with the organizational structure of the public broadcasting system to make it possible to bring leverage to bear locally or regionally on those responsible for programming decisions. The purse-string power thus wielded was as real as any that advertisers had ever exerted on the decision makers of commercial broadcasting. Unless the buffers are strengthened, such an incursion could happen again.

An additional influence on the theoretically unfettered producers of public broadcasting began to develop in recent years as private corporations started making grants to underwrite the costs of specific programs or series on the public broadcasting system. For these grants the corporations did not get the right to hitch commercials to the programs or series; instead they were briefly mentioned as contributors, usually at the beginning and end of a broadcast. They made no sales pitch and on the surface had no control over program content.

But as the practice grew (corporations quickly found it a prestigious form of institutional advertising), the public system became more and more dependent on private grants. Since corporations could decide which programs they wished to underwrite among those on the public broadcasting schedule, they thus acquired an indirect form of influence over programming; corporate grants were not often awarded to fund public affairs or investigative programs dealing with controversial issues.

One way to free public broadcasters from both the threat of occasional government pressure and the side-door influence of corporate grantors would be to provide for the funding of public broadcasting by means of a sequestered tax, perhaps an excise tax earmarked for that purpose. Public radio and television are attracting growing and faithful audiences; that makes the system an ever more tempting target for the various kinds of advertiser counterparts that might hope to manipulate the system for ends other than public service.

MAGAZINES AND ADVERTISERS

Most magazines are proportionately less dependent on advertising revenue than are the broadcast media and the newspapers. The prices paid by subscribers or newsstand purchasers constitute a significant segment (45 to 60 percent) of a magazine's total income.

This seems to suggest that in the media-advertiser relationship magazines ought to be more independent than their counterparts in the other media. But that is too simplistic an analysis. Many magazines may indeed be in a fairly strong position vis-à-vis advertisers, and thus not vulnerable to specific pressures from that quarter; but the reasons for their position of strength are complex and reflect drastic changes in the magazine industry during the last two decades—changes that, in part at least, have been brought about by advertisers.

We have seen how the advent of television resulted in a transformation in the nature of the radio industry. It also had a powerful effect on magazines. As television developed, its ability to deliver mass audiences for an advertiser's message overtook and eventually surpassed that of the remaining national mass medium: the general circulation magazine.

An advertiser who wanted to bring his pitch to the attention of the greatest number of persons at the lowest per-head cost found television a more universal and less costly medium than such magazines as *Collier's, Life,* and *Look.* The magazines edited to have broad, general appeal died off one by one in the face of competition from television; their demise was hastened by the effects of inflation, rising postal costs, and ruinously expensive subscription wars. In the late 1970s few truly generalized magazines were still publishing: *Time, Reader's Digest,* and *Newsweek* were among them.

As the magazines of broad appeal faded from the scene, however, specialized publications proliferated. They survived and prospered despite television and despite rising production and distribution costs because they were able to establish themselves as exclusive or near-exclusive channels of access to *particular* audience segments. Advertisers with a specialized product could be sure of spending their marketing dollars efficiently, reaching only persons with a built-in inclination to buy, when they turned to *Business Week, The New Yorker,* or literally hundreds of other, smaller publications designed to cater intensively—and only—to the interests of boaters, weight watchers, coin collectors, or stereo addicts, for example.

Because specialized magazines represent direct channels to audiences with strong and demonstrated involvement in a specific field or activity, they are invaluable to advertisers with a product or service to sell to such audience segments. And because the readers of such publications are intensely interested in their fields, they are willing to pay relatively high subscription prices, thus leaving the specialized magazine publishers less dependent on advertising revenue. Both factors work to the advantage of the specialized magazines in the media-advertiser relationship.

In sum, advertisers have in recent years profoundly influenced the *overall structure* of the magazine industry, by shifting to television as the preferred medium for the placement of messages designed for the broadest possible audiences. Magazines that attempted to survive as generalized publications encountered increasingly rough going, and many failed. Magazines with appeal for specialized, often narrow audience segments multiplied and prospered. It should be emphasized that this indirect reshaping of the nature of the industry as a whole differs from the specific power plays we have noted in media-advertiser interaction in some of the other media.

The incidence of cases of individual advertisers attempting to obtain free "puff" space or to apply pressure on a magazine to muzzle a story is low. To be sure, evidence here and there suggests that some sort of deal has been struck. Sometimes, for example, an unusually high number of ads from a given industry may appear cozily snuggled around an article dealing with recent developments in that industry. Or a book publisher may tout one of its latest titles in the same issue in which the work is reviewed. These could be coincidental developments, or they could reflect some sort of backstage bargain. But this sort of thing happens far more often in newspaper food, travel, or business sections than it does in magazines; we'll go into that in greater detail later.

When what appears to be a clear-cut instance of advertiser influence over magazine content does show up, it is likely to draw fire from defenders of journalistic tradition. Such a case early in 1976 involved *Esquire* magazine, Xerox Corporation, and a distinguished, retired *New Yorker* writer.

Xerox had proposed to the editors of *Esquire* that the corporation sponsor a major article in the magazine. The article would be written by Harrison Salisbury of the *New York Times,* and it could be on whatever subject Salisbury and the magazine's editors agreed would be acceptable. Xerox would not dictate the nature of the piece. The company would pay Salisbury $55,000 for writing the article, but would exercise no supervision or control over its content. After the article had been finished and accepted by *Esquire* for publication, Xerox would have the right to place advertising both before and after the article, indicating its sponsorship of the piece. If for any reason Xerox chose not to associate itself with the article, it need not run the ads; but the understanding was that in other issues of *Esquire* the company would place at least $115,000 worth of advertising.

The Xerox officials who developed the proposal emphasized that they didn't want to establish specifications for the article in any way, nor did they want to meddle with *Esquire*'s editorial policies. Their sole purpose was to provide funding for a high-quality article by a respected writer—an article that otherwise might never be written or published. The Xerox officials noted that the firm had sponsored major television documentaries on the same basis, without any control over the content, and with the purpose of improving the quality of TV programming—and the additional purpose, of course, of placing Xerox in a favorable light as the underwriter of programs of substance. The magazine venture would be analogous.

The editors of *Esquire* found the proposition reasonable, as did Salisbury. He researched and wrote the article, "Travels Through America," and it was duly published in the February 1976 issue of *Esquire.*

Shortly thereafter, E. B. White, once one of the brightest names on *The New Yorker* staff and now living in retirement in a New England village, wrote a letter to the editor of his local paper. He protested the Xerox-*Esquire*-Salisbury arrangement as a threat to journalistic standards and press freedom. Because White is one of the most respected figures in contemporary American journalism and literature, his relatively brief but biting comment came to the attention of Xerox officials. They were troubled by his position, and one of them wrote to ask why he saw such evil in a carefully safeguarded, straightforward sponsorship arrangement. There followed an exchange of letters and an eventual decision by Xerox to abandon the whole idea, even though several other sponsored articles were by then on the drawing boards.

White's persuasive argument centered on the theme of integrity:

> I see something ominous and unhealthy when a corporation underwrites an article in a magazine of general circulation. . . . Whenever money changes hands, something goes along with it—an intangible something that varies with the circumstances. . . . Sponsorship in the press is an invitation to corruption and abuse. . . .[9]

SUMMARY

In the foregoing passages we have traced how advertisers try to influence the nature and content of various communication media by exploiting the bottom-line factor. By no means have we exhausted the topic. In the context of a compact overview, we can deal with illustrative instances but we cannot offer a comprehensive analysis.

No single pattern has emerged from our examination. The opportunity to exert influence varies, we have found, from medium to medium, and also within a given medium as factors of size, competition, and tradition come into play. The several ways in which the media have evolved historically have helped to determine their varying degrees of vulnerability.

It does seem clear, however, that the advertiser—the principal source of revenue for most of the media—does indeed have some hand in shaping the nonadvertising content of the final media products. The shaping is not necessarily sinister or subversive. The advertiser's leverage may be applied indirectly more often than directly. But the advertiser-media relationship undoubtedly is one of the factors that determine how the media depict the world around us and provide us with intimations of reality.

In the course of our exploration of the media-advertiser relationship, it has been apparent that the degree to which advertisers are effective in shaping the media may depend as much on the backbone and sense of responsibility of the media managers as on the clout or motivation of the advertiser. So let's consider next how the bottom-line factor affects owners of the media and determines their approach to their role in making the media tick.

3
The Role
of Ownership

Whether his or her title is owner, publisher, network president, or station manager, no individual associated with a media enterprise is as conscious of the importance of the bottom line as is the person who makes the final decisions.

The top management figure is the one held accountable if the balance sheet shows red. It is the publisher (or network president, or station manager) who must decide priorities and allocate resources between those aspects of the operation that generate revenue (advertising, time sales, circulation) and those that spend it (newspaper and magazine editorial staffs, broadcasting programmers and news teams, and the production crews in all media).

Ideally, this delicate balancing act will be performed with the dual objective of turning out a media product attractive enough to hold an audience that advertisers will pay to reach, yet also substantial enough to provide consumers with the news and information that they need to function as members of the community. "Attractive" and "substantial" are not synonymous. Any media proprietor is well aware of that, and also of the consequences of shifting emphasis from one to the other.

Many members of the consuming public are also aware of these considerations. One of the most frequently voiced criticisms of the press is that "they'll print anything just to sell a few more papers." Another: "Of course there's sex and violence on TV—they'll run as much as they can get away with, just to drum up an audience."

So let's look into how "they" really make their choices. Are media managers obsessed with maximizing earnings, and do they let this factor shape the nature of the media product?

Do publishers and network news executives understand and respect the public service obligations of the media they direct? Do they give those obligations full measure, or only pious lip service?

What differences are there among the media managers' attitudes toward their jobs, and why do those differences exist?

Just how decisive is the role of ownership in making the media tick, in determining how well we are being served by the newspapers, magazines, and broadcast outlets that are our only windows on the world?

Before going on, let's define briefly what is meant by "public service obligations" of the news media, since this is the factor that distinguishes the media from other kinds of businesses and necessitates the balancing act for their owners.

In earlier eras those who were interested in the press and its role talked less about obligations than about freedom. The First Amendment said nothing about responsibilities; it spelled out the necessity for the press to be free of government control. It reflected the libertarian concept of the press that was then in vogue and remained so for more than a century thereafter. This concept held that the interests of the public would be best served if the press were entirely free to print whatever it pleased. (In those days, of course, print was the only medium.) If such freedom were safeguarded, so the libertarians reasoned, then all views and opinions would have a chance to be known and evaluated by the public, and out of these diverse and contending voices truth would eventually emerge.

The libertarian theory was logical and appealing, considering the history of the press up to that time. Absolute rulers had muzzled and threatened the press, allowing only pro-government expressions. The libertarians felt it essential to guarantee all voices a chance to be heard and specifically to prohibit government from silencing or harassing any of them, loyal or dissident.

Underlying the libertarian theory, however, was an assumption that there would always be many different press voices, and that all segments of the public would have access to the various expressions flowing from them. This was not a wholly valid assumption even in that distant era. True enough, there were numerous newspapers, pamphleteers, and broadside writers. But not everyone, even then, was able to muster the funds to get into print. And literacy was far from universal.

As the American press evolved, the libertarian assumptions became less and less applicable. Today the media channels are few in number, considering the vast population of the country. And access to those channels is extremely costly, whether we are talking about acquiring ownership control of one of them or simply purchasing space or time for the ventilation of personal viewpoints.

In recognition of the changed circumstances, press theorists proposed modifications of the libertarian concept. Keep the First Amendment freedom from government control, by all means; but graft to the freedom a sense of responsibility. Since the media channels now are few, and in the control of a tiny proportion of our population, those who do control the channels should acknowledge their obligation to provide a comprehensive, balanced report of the news.

The libertarians asked no such obligation of the press of their day; editors didn't have to be factual, unbiased, or objective. It was vital only that they be free; out of that freedom, and the diversity of views expressed, a reliable impression of reality would be discernible.

Now, however, the social responsibility theorists argue that we can't afford to tolerate bias, distortion, or imbalance in the few media channels that remain; the public should be able to have confidence that those who control the media will respect the obligation to inform the public fully and accurately. Of course, this is a nonenforceable obligation; the First Amendment hasn't been revamped to incorporate it. The social responsibility theorists expect the media managers to accept the obligation voluntarily. Most do, some more whole-heartedly and conscientiously than others.

BALANCING THE SCALES

If we make the assumption that most media owners today at least are aware of the social responsibility concept, how defensibly do they strike a balance between their understandable concern to keep the enterprise solvent and in economic good health and their presumed desire to fulfill the public service obligations?

In trying to identify the extent of advertiser influence we discovered that all of the media cannot be considered in generic terms; they differ from medium to medium, and there are all shapes and sizes within a given medium. It is necessary to make similar distinctions in considering how and why ownership forces mold the media.

We can begin with some general observations, however. One is that all of those who make the final decisions on newspapers, magazines, or in broadcasting are well aware of the consequences of shifting emphasis from one pan of the balancing scales to the other.

Newspaper editors know that if their sole objective is to make a paper that will earn maximum profits, they need only load its columns with human interest stories, cut out costly investigative series and public service crusades, and reserve plenty of space for the advertisers attracted by the rising circulation. Some do exactly that.

Television network presidents and individual station owners know that they can fatten the black figures on the balance sheet by maintaining time-tested programming formulas, hyping the ratings by adroit juggling of time slots, and scrupulously avoiding controversial—and costly—news documentaries. Some do exactly that.

At what point on the media spectrum is there evidence of a "profits-first" mentality in control? Where—and why—are there instances in which a more responsible balance appears to have been struck between economic necessity and public obligation? Let's look at newspapers first, as we did in the earlier discussion of advertiser influence.

There are some easy targets. The *National Enquirer* has loaded the scale so heavily on the side of trivia and sensationalism that virtually no pretense of public service obligation is evident.

Rupert Murdoch, the Australian who has built an international newspaper empire (including, as of 1976, the *New York Post*), deals frankly and openly in sensationalism as a means of building and holding circulation.

The *New York Daily News*, America's largest newspaper in terms of circulation, serves up big helpings of sex, crime, and gossip, plenty of arresting pictures, and only limited rations of solid news. In the process it outsells all the competition in New York (though Murdoch's *Post* may give it a run for the money).

These papers (the *Enquirer* more than the others) represent holdovers from an era of yellow journalism during which such figures as William Randolph Hearst and Bernarr Macfadden (publisher of the *New York Evening Graphic*, tagged by critics as the "Pornographic") strove to outdo each other in jazzing up and trivializing the news. Battling for circulation, they believed that they were giving the public what it wanted. Whether the public was getting the kind of news it *needed* was not particularly important to the yellow journalists.

Unhappily, there is evidence of a partial revival of the philosophy of those bad old days. In a discussion of what they termed "The New Ballyhoo!!!" the editors of *Columbia Journalism Review* recently cited

> the decision of a few major papers to subordinate deliberately news of public affairs in favor of sensation. *The San Francisco Chronicle* pioneered in this pattern more than 15 years ago; now it has been joined, in intent if not in execution, by such papers as *The Detroit News* and *The Cincinnati Post*.[10]

The *Review* editors applied to this neosensationalism the slogan, "All the news that sells."

No one would contend that this neosensationalism compares with the wide-open days of yellow journalism. But why is there even a pale revival of a discredited era in American press history? Competitive pressures appear to account at least in part for the trend. For years public opinion polls have been recording the increasing dependence of large segments of the population on television as their chief source of news. This pattern has caused discomfiture and concern among newspaper managers. Although industry statisticians demonstrated that a majority of the public still turned to newspapers for local news and ads, and for extended detail on national and international stories, the steadily increasing dominance of television as the overall source of news worried the publishers.

Newspapers do not compete with television so directly as do the general circulation magazines; newspapers are local media, and much of television is national in character. Still, newspapers have felt the bite of the TV competition even on the local scene. What should be done about those bothersome poll figures?

Some editors and publishers decided they ought to challenge TV on its own ground. They would beef up the entertainment content of their papers, using more features, pictures, human interest news; they would try for a magazine look in makeup. And, at least in some cases, they would bring back the days of Ballyhoo!!!

Not all papers took this tack, by any means. And many editors warned that it was exactly the wrong way to go—to pick a fight on the opponent's own ground.

Ralph Sewell, who spent a lifetime as an Oklahoma editor, warned his colleagues that they were over-reacting to television and were becoming more superficial in the process. His advice: forget the gimmickry and get back to providing the news.[11] In effect Sewell was calling for the newspaper managers to even the unbalanced scales, to live up to the obligation to provide the public with the news it *needs* to have, not just the news it appears to *want* to have.

Yet economic and competitive considerations continue to influence editors and publishers to gamble on the tactic of tilting in the direction of reader appeal—give them what they want, jazz it up—in the hope of stemming TV's gains.

Nor has the gambit been confined to just a few newspapers; those few have gone overboard, but many others have also begun to experiment. Edwin Diamond, a commentator for the *Washington Post*'s radio and television stations, points to the rapid emergence of unabashed gossip columns in many papers (including the *Post*, the *The New York Times*, even *Women's Wear Daily*).

> There is an apparently insatiable desire for "items" about "beautiful people" and public figures alike. Sensing this, the gossip machinery of the press works around the clock to feed the appetite. The normal rules of journalism are often suspended.[12]

However, this is only one way in which the influence of the bottom line on publishers helps to shape the nature of the newspaper. Another is evident in the products of some newspaper chains, or groups as they now prefer to be termed.

Some chain owners, as we noted in the case of Lord Thomson, are interested chiefly in the money-making potential of their properties. However, the degree to which a profits-first philosophy filters down from central ownership to individual publishers or editors in the group varies considerably from one group to another. The heads of the Gannett group, for example, are undoubtedly interested in showing a healthy balance sheet to the group's stockholders; yet there is little evidence that Gannett management demands corner cutting or subordination of the public service obligation of its member newspapers in order to maximize profits. The same could be said for the Ottaway group, the *New York Times* group, and the Knight-Ridder group.

In other groups, however, it is nakedly obvious that the choice has been made to put profits above all else, including social responsibility. This is more likely to be true of groups of relatively small dailies than of the big metropolitan combinations. In some (again, not all) of these small-paper groups the news hole is filled as inexpensively as possible, with wire service and syndicated copy. Local news, which is costly by comparison since it must be gathered by the paper's own staff, is held to a minimum. That leaves plenty of room for advertising. It also tilts the scales heavily away from the public service obligation.

The emphasis on profits at the expense of quality journalistic service to the community is not characteristic only of group newspapers, to be sure. Many of the nation's finest newspapers belong to groups: some of the sorriest sheets are in the hands of independent owners. In fact, it has many times been demonstrated that takeover by a group with enlightened central management can represent a step forward rather than backward for the journalistic quality of a formerly independently owned paper.

Groups can bring an outside perspective that can cut through encrusted relationships and archaic practices that inhibit forceful and comprehensive news coverage on some ingrown, home-owned papers. Groups can provide cost-saving central purchasing and accounting services, thus freeing more money for the editorial side. Groups can offer the financial depth that can underwrite plant automation and—more importantly—reduce the vulnerability of an individual publisher to various pressures, including those of advertisers. So there *are* advantages to be had from group membership—always provided that the central management of the group is alive to the necessity to produce good journalism as well as up-to-date and profitable media products.

With these points acknowledged, it is nonetheless necessary to add that group ownership, *as a system*, does tend to encourage a profits-first philosophy in the office of the top decision maker on the scene. The group publisher is not the owner; he works for a corporate headquarters, for a set of stockholders. Sometimes newspaper groups are parts of vast industrial conglomerates, with holdings in many fields. It's easy to see how the journalistic ideal of informing the people fully and fairly might get short shrift in such a set of relationships.

The manager of an individual store in a drugstore chain works to build profits and win points at the chain headquarters; a group publisher may experience pressure to take a similar tack, even if this requires some corner cutting and shortchanging in carrying out the public service obligations of the paper.

The independent owner-publisher is likely to be closely involved with his publication. As a member of the community the independent publisher is probably concerned that the paper serve the public interest as well as provide a comfortable profit. This isn't true of all independents, but of a great many.

Among the smallest papers, the country weeklies, there are more independent owners than group members, although the number of groups is steadily growing. Here, too, there is a wide range of performance. Many country editors diligently mine the news of their communities and give the readers a full local roundup. Some other small-town publishers see their properties as business ventures primarily; they fill the pages with ''boiler plate'' (preprinted or canned material from syndicates, bought for a song) and turn out products that are little more than shoppers. Many of them make a mint at it.

One bit of evidence of the tendency for community publishers to keep an eye on the main chance cropped up during the 1976 political campaign. The *Nashville Banner* surveyed a number of Tennessee weekly newspapers and found that more than half had a policy of not reporting that local candidates were running for office unless the candidates were willing to pay for the articles at advertising rates, or would take out paid political announcements. Here, obviously, the public service role was subordinate, with economic considerations literally shaping the nature of the news.[13]

THE BRIGHTER SIDE

Happily, there are many newspapers in this country where management policy firmly and deliberately tilts the scales on the side of public service.

The *New York Times* makes a very small profit on its newspaper properties, by design. The money is plowed back into the operation, invested in news staff and news coverage. The family-owned *Times* makes a profit on other, related enterprises owned by the corporation, including newsprint mills. But so far as the newspaper is concerned, high-quality journalism and sensitivity to the social responsibility concept come first and the ledger sheets second. A similar philosophy dominates the *Washington Post,* owned by Katharine Graham; the *Los Angeles Times*, operated by the Chandler family; and the *Louisville Courier-Journal*, operated by the Bingham family. All four publications routinely appear on lists of the ''greatest'' or ''finest'' or ''best'' American papers, and the citations are deserved.

But it is not only among the journalistic giants that the public service obligation is respected. Admirable performances are evident in many smaller, less well-known newspapers, among them the *Riverside* (California) *Press-Enterprise,* the *Charlotte* (North Carolina) *Observer*, the *Eugene* (Oregon)

Register-Guard, and the *St. Petersburg* (Florida) *Times*. Two of the four (Eugene and Riverside) are independently owned and two are associated with newspaper groups. Their circulations range from 50,000 to 188,000. Pound for pound, they measure up to the *Times* of New York or of Los Angeles in terms of quality. And the priorities are on public service, not profit.

There are others like them—far too many to list—among the nation's 1760 dailies. (That figure is an average; during the last ten years the number has varied from a low of 1748 to a high of 1774, but the variation has been up and down; no single trend is evident.) I would not venture to guess what percentage of that number represents publications whose ownership is concerned more for journalistic integrity than for the bottom line, and what percentage represents those on which profits come first and the news is shaped to fit. There is a spectrum, as we have seen. The best and worst cases are fairly readily identifiable, but there is a large middle band. In which direction and at what angle the scales tip on those publications may not be at once apparent to the outside observer. My own view is that the "good guys" far outnumber those in the black hats.

ON THE BROADCASTING FRONT

In the news programming of the broadcast media—radio and television—there are parallels to most of the situations we have been examining in the last few pages.

The counterpart of the newspaper owner who cuts corners on news and public service to swell profits is the station manager who opts for a "rip and read" approach to news coverage, in which announcers or newscasters simply read brief segments from the wire service reports, and little or no staff coverage of news is undertaken.

The preoccupation of some editors with a Ballyhoo!!! or neosensationalist approach to the news is matched by broadcast owners who go all out for high ratings by adopting the "happy talk" format for their news shows. This format, developed and promoted by broadcast consultant firms, calls for lively banter among the newscasters, heavy emphasis on stories of violence and sex, and a drastic paring down of the time allotted to any single news item.

A CBS "Sixty Minutes" program surveyed the "happy talk" phenomenon and quoted the following excerpts from one newscast on KGO-TV, San Francisco, "one of the highest-rated" (audience ratings, that is) in the country:

> And the latest on the little old lady who looked at the nude male fold-outs of Jim Brown and Jon Davidson, and said—The full story—next—right here, on Channel 7 "News Scene."

(Laughter)

The exorcism craze and scare is spreading all over this country right now. Tonight, a band of young churchgoers (singing "Onward, Christian Soldiers") burned 40 books on the occult, plus a Ouija board in Rock Island, Illinois.

Coming up, the mother of a nude talks about her son—barely.

The wife of the ex-mayor of St. Augustine, Florida, was killed in front of her home. She died—screaming for help on her front porch . . . [murdered] by a man who, police say, may have hacked her to death out of simple pure hate. . . .[14]

Stations that accept the consultants' advice to adopt "happy talk" typically boost their Nielsen ratings dramatically and cut into the standings of competing stations that stick with a more traditional—and more responsible—approach. The bottom line clearly has priority with ownership willing to warp the news into the "happy talk" format. A top-rated news show can produce half or more of a station's profit.

Some TV news reporters have been outspoken in their resentment of the practice of making performers of anchorpersons and trivializing and sensationalizing the broadcast news report. One highly successful young anchorman says, "The only reason to call the show I'm on 'news' is that the title of it is 'Eyewitness News.' It's really an entertainment program, and what they want of me is to be a literate buffoon."[15] And Charles Kuralt of the CBS "On the Road" reports told a meeting of radio and television news directors that

I don't care what the station managers say, I don't care what the outside professional news advisers say, I don't care what the ratings say, I say this is a continuing disgrace of this profession. The plain truth is that in a society which depends for its life on an informed citizenry, and in which most citizens receive most of their information from television, millions are getting that life-giving information from a man, or a woman, whose colleagues wouldn't trust [him or her] to accurately report on his or her afternoon round of golf.[16]

Fortunately, just as there are plenty of good newspapers to cite despite the tactics of the minority, so are there also instances of notably comprehensive and responsible news handling to note on both radio and television.

The CBS "Sixty Minutes" show has maintained for a half-dozen years a high level of quality in its investigative reporting, as did NBC's "First Tuesday" during the years it was on the air. The nightly national news shows on all three networks have provided brief but straightforward treatment of the major news stories of the day. And individual stations, such as WCKT-TV, Miami; WPVI-TV, Philadelphia; and WNET, the New York public television outlet, have turned in outstanding work on documentaries.

Many local stations, in fact, do a better job in that area than do the networks, where documentaries have been fewer and fewer in recent years. Marlene Sanders, ABC's vice president in charge of documentaries, says, "Every time I go into a corporate meeting, there are great sighs and groans. Every network feels that way—the documentary is merely tolerated.'' The network attitude toward the documentaries, contends *Newsweek,* is primarily the result of its ''bottom-line mentality.'' Documentaries draw smaller audiences than prime-time entertainment series and, thus, alienate advertisers interested only in profits.[17]

Yet the ''bottom-line mentality'' certainly did not prevail when network executives took over huge chunks of valuable air time to make the Watergate and impeachment committee hearings available to the public. The networks gave up hundreds of thousands of dollars worth of programming every day to perform a notable public service. That was surely at the other end of the scale from the ratings-hungry approach of the ''happy talk'' shows. The networks similarly provided valuable time for the 1976 election campaign debates between the presidential and vice presidential candidates. This was not so massive a time commitment as was involved in the Watergate and impeachment coverage, but it was plucked from the very middle of the choicest and most costly prime broadcast time.

How can we sum up broadcasting and the bottom line? One of the most knowledgeable observers of the two electronic media is Marvin Barrett, editor of the biennial Columbia-DuPont surveys. In Barrett's midterm interim report covering much of 1974 and 1975, his concluding thumbnail assessment of what he found is as useful as any, reflecting as it does the mixed nature of the media:

> The messages that the nation's broadcasters beamed to the American people were paradoxical and difficult of application. Embedded in a continuum of trash, the signals of the journalists were all too brief and frequently adulterated by their surroundings. Still, the same journalists had helped bring to light and terminate the national scandal of Watergate, the international horror of Vietnam. Now, lacking a subject of such dramatic proportions, they were once more occupying themselves with the continuing failure of the republic to cope with the country around it, its deteriorating environment, its shrinking resources, its floundering economy, its old, its mentally and physically handicapped, its criminal and violent, its minorities, its poor. . . . When, in the fall of 1975, prime-time TV viewing was reported to have declined by 6 per cent, the news ratings, significantly, remained firm.[18]

Finally, Av Westin, former ABC vice president for news, has commented that since television is regarded as an entertainment medium, this affects the way information is presented; because television is ''show business,'' television news is a part of show business.[19]

AND, FINALLY, MAGAZINES

It is difficult to analyze how much ownership preoccupation with profits shapes the news offered by magazines. There are literally thousands of magazines, virtually all designed primarily for narrow, specialized audiences. The readership target may be the workers in a given industry, as is the case with house organs or industrial magazines; or it may be a cross section of persons who share a devotion to fly-tying, or motorcycles, or stamp-collecting. Each specialized magazine contains news of interest to the particular readership that the magazine seeks to reach. But these magazines cannot be considered on the same plane as newspapers designed for general circulation in a community, or TV programs developed to serve a whole city or the nation.

There are also "think" magazines, devoted primarily to opinion but also carrying news deliberately selected to appeal to a like-thinking group of readers of a certain political persuasion (*Nation, National Review, New Republic*, and others).

There are magazines for regional audiences of a special kind (*Arizona Highways, Sunset*); others with an emphasis on matters literary (*Atlantic, Harper's, Saturday Review*); and yet others that cater to somewhat different sets of tastes (*Playboy, Hustler, Playgirl*). None of these is a true news medium, comparable to the general circulation newspaper or the broadcast news programs, even though all have *some* news content. In each instance they are designed to meet the needs of an audience segment and thus deliberately aim to give the readers what they want, not to provide a balanced picture of the world.

A few magazines might appropriately be categorized as general news-magazines, though even in their case the label is subject to some qualification. These include *Time, Newsweek*, and *U.S. News and World Report*. Certain other, specialized magazines, even though their content is primarily news *(Business Week, Forbes, Fortune),* fall outside the small circle of general news-magazines.

If we concern ourselves only with those magazines that are most nearly comparable with the other news media we have been considering, and then try to assess how their owners appear to be balancing public service against the maximizing of profits, we can draw few conclusions with confidence. The evidence upon which to base such conclusions is scanty.

Our problem arises partly because the newsmagazines tend to blend news and opinion so skillfully that sorting out the constituent elements is not easy, whereas the newspapers and the broadcast media make a good faith effort, at least, to keep news and opinion separate.

If we accept the newsmagazines on their own terms, setting aside the news-opinion mixing to be dealt with later, we can attempt a few generalized judgments.

The newsmagazines do, for example, touch the bases comprehensively. The news report compiled on a weekly rather than a daily deadline is sometimes much more perceptive and focused than the daily installments in the newspaper or on the broadcast media. Both *Time* and *Newsweek* provide their readers with occasional thoroughly researched and reported stories that constitute public service of a high order (such as a series of Bicentennial commentaries by representative Americans or a searching look at the origins and record of Jimmy Carter as he suddenly emerged as the Democratic candidate for president). *U.S. News and World Report* uses graphs, tables, and interviews with experts to illuminate some of the murky economic issues of the time. *The National Observer*, before it folded in mid-1977, regularly tackled complex and thoughtful subjects (the ethics of various professional groups; the ''death with dignity'' issue).

However, close assay of the newsmagazines' content also reveals material patently included to snag reader attention and build circulation. The *National Observer* devoted pages of its newspaper-size format to recounting the ludicrous antics of a staff member attempting to compete in an Alaskan dog race, or to sail a small craft around the globe. And both *Time* and *Newsweek* have increasingly tended to emphasize superficial personality news and sensationalism, as has been the case with some newspapers.

Time even spawned a new magazine dedicated wholly to the exploitation of fluff and gossip—*People*—and saw its offspring zoom to a circulation of a million and a half in less than a year on a formula of brief personality sketches, piquant gossip, and lots of pictures. This was an obvious exploitation of the superficial, a partial return to a Ballyhoo!!! philosophy, and pretty clear evidence that in this instance, at least, public service obligation took a distant second place to maximized profits.

In brief, the picture is mixed. Considering the fight for survival that all general circulation magazines are making against TV competition—the newsmagazines as·well as the others—it would be surprising if we did *not* find concessions being made to the need for attracting and holding circulation. Perhaps it is an encouraging sign that the major newsmagazines are as balanced and comprehensive as they are, and that the instances of clear-cut ownership preoccupation with the bottom line are not more frequent.

SUMMARY

In nearly all the media of mass communication that offer news as one of the significant elements of their overall package, the concern of ownership with the bottom line is among the factors that shape the end product.

There are a few exceptions, in the form of small opinion magazines that are subsidized by a wealthy owner as a kind of hobby or mission; or in the form of radio and television stations that operate on the basis of voluntary subscriptions or contributions from listeners or viewers. But most media are business ventures; their owners are acutely conscious of that fact. Some owners are equally conscious of their public service obligation, and balance the scales at a responsible angle. They try to cope as best they can with the dilemma inherent in any news enterprise. Ben H. Bagdikian, the foremost media critic of our day, was talking specifically about newspapers in the following paragraphs, but the situation he describes has its parallel in all of the other news media:

> On the one hand, the daily paper in the United States is a product of professionals whose reporting is supposed to be the result of disciplined intelligence gathering and analysis in order to present an honest and understandable picture of the social and political world. If this reportage is in any way influenced by concern for money-making it is regarded as corrupt journalism.
>
> On the other hand, the American daily newspaper, like any other business enterprise, has to remain solvent and has to make a profit or else it will not survive. If it doesn't make money there will be no reporting of any kind, ethical or unethical. If the corporate end of the enterprise does not have an effective concern for making money it will be regarded by everyone, including journalists, as incompetent, negligent and a disservice to its community.
>
> As a result of these opposing goals we have in the 1,770 dailies and 8,000 weeklies two groups under the same roof, one under severe demands to ignore profits on pain of condemnation for corruption, and the other under similarly severe demands to make a profit on pain of being considered stupid.[20]

We have seen in the several chapters in this section how the urgent realities of the bottom line are reconciled with the social responsibility of the news media to inform the public. The reconciliation is achieved with varying degrees of success in the several media, and among individual enterprises in a single medium. Beyond question, however, economic considerations are among the forces that make the media tick. In the next section we'll look at some others of those forces.

SECTION TWO
NEWSPEOPLE
AND
NEWS SOURCES

During the discussion in section 1 of the ways that economic considerations influence how the media tick, there were occasional echoes of conflicts between management and staff, or between media people and the persons in the community with whom they come into contact. Not always are rank-and-file members of a news media organization fully satisfied with the way ownership seeks to balance economic survival against public service obligations. And not always are news media representatives on congenial terms with the officials or private citizens from whom they must gather the news. The kinds of relationships that build up within news media organizations, and between those organizations and other elements in the community, can significantly determine how the media function.

In this section we shall look first at the relationships *within* the news media, between owners and staff members, between editors and reporters or newscasters. These relationships inevitably mold or color the nature of the news media products that eventually come to our attention. We shall also look at the complex and varied web of relationships that grows up between the persons who staff the news media and the many individuals in the community with whom they must interact during their daily efforts to discover, report, and disseminate the news. How these relationships build and change, and what pressures they exert on the persons who staff the news media, shape the way the news is perceived, first by the media and in turn by those of us who are dependent on the media for our visions of reality.

4
Tugs and Tensions Within

MOTIVATIONS

Let's begin with an examination of the motivations that actuate persons in the news business, apart from the obvious desire to make a living. There are several such motivations. Some media people respond to all of them, others to only one or two.

Ego Satisfaction

Each of us needs to find a means of self-expression. There is a powerful psychic return to the person who sees his or her writing going out daily to 200,000 newspaper readers, or becoming part of the nightly newscast viewed by half a million. CBS network newsman Daniel Schorr was suspended from his job for a number of weeks while a controversy between Schorr and a congressional committee over concealment of news sources wound to a conclusion. Later Schorr acknowledged that it had been rough to forego the daily "fix" he experienced from getting a story on the air. "I wondered," he said, "if I could get along without it."[1] (Apparently he decided he could, since he resigned his CBS job shortly thereafter; however, he turned to print journalism for another variety of "fix.")

Many newswriters share Schorr's feeling. The sense of exultation and satisfaction deriving from the sight of your by-line on a page one story, or from the sight of the camera's red eye winking on as you begin a report to network millions about a news development you have covered that day—is indeed a "high." The daily pursuit of such heady satisfaction gives meaning to the work of many persons in the news business.

There are comparable rewards, though less personal and intense, to the desk editor who proudly surveys the headlines and page makeup of the day's issue, or to the TV producer who finally relaxes in that busy seat before the bank of monitors as a deftly crafted nightly news show is wrapped up, or to the newsmagazine writer who finds his or her name among those listed at the end of a group story as contributors.

The ego-satisfaction factor keeps women and men in the news business despite their awareness that they could do better financially, or work at a more congenial pace, in some other line of activity. That factor also leads some newspeople to build up a story to make sure that it will get into the paper, to search for an arresting angle so that the article will make page one, or to pad the account so that it will seem impressive enough to warrant a by-line. The hungry need for the daily "fix" can lead reporters to sensationalize and columnists to grab at unverified "scoops." It can lead newscasters to search for action stories with movement and violence, at the expense of more static but perhaps more consequential accounts. But such abuses are not the norm. The typical man or woman in the news business responds to ego motivation, certainly, but not by exceeding the reportorial role. For another, equally strong motivating factor for news people is public service.

Public Service

Those at the cutting edge of media enterprises—the reporters and camera people who are covering the stories on the spot, and their colleagues who process the copy and film back in the shop—are fully as conscious of the social responsibility concept as are the editors, publishers, and station managers (much *more* conscious, in many cases).

It may not be statistically provable, but it is nonetheless a fact that a strong streak of idealism runs through most working newspersons. It is conventional wisdom that reporters grow into hardened cynics as the years go by, ready to believe the worst of everyone. But scratch just about any of those cynics and you'll uncover a lively sense of the journalistic ethic, a quick response to the thesis that the true role of the press is to serve the public interest by making available as honest and as full a report of the news as it is humanly possible to assemble.

Newsmen and newswomen typically are deadly serious about their public service obligation, because they do believe in it and because belief in it invests their role with a special cachet; as agents of the public weal, they are more than job holders. They are professionals whose efforts are important to the functioning of our system of representative government.

Admittedly, for some reporters and others connected with the news media, public service is not a motivation. But they aren't typical, any more than are those who twist the ego-satisfaction factor out of shape.

Being in the Middle of Things

Most of us take satisfaction from being where the action is. Reporters and other newspeople know more about what's going on in the community or the nation than do the rest of us. They are there when a president stumbles, when a district attorney lets his or her hair down after a case is finished, when a five-alarm fire guts half of downtown. They are privy to more details than get into the paper or on the air.

Someone who is not a journalist but chances to be on the scene when an accident takes place knows the feeling of temporary importance, of responding to friends' eager queries, of recounting over and over the special shock and immediacy generated by the experience. This is the stuff of daily life to the reporter or editor.

To be sure, some of that daily life can be tedious, some of it uncomfortably grisly or distressing. But overall the sense of being in the middle of momentous action; of interacting with the news figures of the community, the nation, or the world; of being one-up, in a sense, on all the lesser-informed— this is an aspect of the life of the newsperson that few would willingly give up. For many, it is a compelling reason for entering and staying in the field.

For some others, a similarly attractive reason for being in journalism is the opportunity it offers to wield power.

Power

The group of media persons one first thinks of in connection with the power motivation is the owners, publishers, and managers of the various mass communication enterprises.

Newspaper publishers and TV station managers are obviously persons to be reckoned with in the community—and they very well know it.

For publishers, times have changed somewhat and the significance of editorial endorsements of candidates has been downgraded by the results of research. (However, a recent study by a University of Michigan researcher revives the notion that newspaper endorsements do make a significant difference in the outcome of political campaigns, even in this TV age.)[2]

Yet the power of publishers or of broadcast media managers is by no means confined to the sphere of politics. There is real, crucial power in the hands of the person who makes the final decisions about what news and what opinion will go out to the reading or viewing public, and which will end up in the newsroom wastebasket or on the cutting-room floor. The choice of what news and what impressions go out through the media and which remain non-news helps to shape the agenda of public discussion and thus, ultimately, the march of events.

The acme of media power is perhaps that wielded by the oracular figures at center stage: the TV anchorpersons, the leading syndicated columnists, the editorial writers for such reverberating voices as the *New York Times.*

Only half jocularly, Newbold Noyes, former editor of the *Washington Star,* made the following observation before the 1976 presidential campaign:

> I was having lunch the other day with a group of news executives in Washington, and the talk turned to what was likely to happen at the Democratic Convention next year. "It will all depend," one of us said, "on the reaction of someone who is in constant contact with all those delegates—someone they trust who's not directly involved in the partisan fighting—Walter Cronkite." Well, maybe that's pushing it a little too far. Maybe Walter alone can't decide who will be nominated. But can anyone doubt that the news media as a whole—all the TV anchormen and commentators, all the newspaper reporters and columnists and editorial writers—will as a group have more to do with what happens in any convention, or in any election, than any other forces extant?[3]

But the power of the mass media is not alone in the hands of the mega-stars, or the moneybags.

In *The Boys on the Bus*, Timothy Crouse describes in vivid, convincing detail how the political reporters covering the 1972 primary campaigns for the presidential nominations were in fact the persons who orchestrated the development of those campaigns and in significant measure determined their outcome.

> By reporting a man's political strengths, they make him a front runner; by mentioning his weaknesses and liabilities, they cut him down. . . . The press was no longer guessing who might run and who might win; the press was in some way determining these things. . . .[4]

Similar leverage is in the hands of *all* media persons in varying degrees; it isn't limited to nightly news personages, powerful publishers, or the reporters on the campaign buses. Every reporter, whether for the *Grand Forks* (North Dakota) *Herald* or the *Washington Post*, whether for a small market radio station or the CBS network, is at the cutting edge of the news, where initial decisions are made about what events or aspects of a situation will enter the flow of the news and which will wither away, unknown and unseen, because a reporter left them out of the story, or a camera person turned the lens another direction.

Reporters and other newspeople are keenly aware of this power and of their obligation to use it responsibly—as most of them do. News sources are equally aware of the power in the hands of those who will report their utterances and activities. Anyone who has ever made a speech or issued a press release has agonized afterward, waiting to see how much of it, and what parts, would get through the reportorial screen and out to the public. Would it be a representative report, or one focused on the superficial rather than the substantive? Would the speaker be made to sound knowing, or foolish? Would the photographer select a shot that showed the candidate picking his nose, or looking dignified?

In *The Boys on the Bus* Crouse recounts a revealing episode during the 1972 primary campaign of Senator Edmund Muskie, the front runner at the time. The New Hampshire primary was over and Muskie had won with a 46 percent plurality. The reporters, however, who had predicted that he would garner 50 percent, wrote that he hadn't done as well as expected. Then a reporter asked Muskie how the New Hampshire results would affect his chances in subsequent primaries.

> "I can't tell you that," Muskie snapped. "You'll tell me and you'll tell the rest of the country because you interpret this victory. This press conference today is my only chance to interpret it, but you'll probably even misinterpret that."[5]

The disappointed, angry outburst from the senator was overstatment; but there was truth in it. The power of the people in the news media is a solid reality from which there is usually little effective appeal.

Awareness of the opportunity to wield such power is one of the motivating factors for reporters, editors, newscasters, camera people, and media managers. In few other careers can you so quickly move into a position in which your actions and decisions can affect in so many ways the lives and hopes of your fellows.

ROLES IN THE NEWSROOM

The various motivations of newspeople—ego satisfaction, public service, being in the center of events, and wielding power—all obviously play a part in making the media tick, shaping the picture of the world that comes to us from those media. The ways in which these motivations are relatively effective in molding the news are in turn determined to some degree by interrelationships within the newsgathering and -disseminating organizations themselves.

One of the leading sociologists of our time, Morris Janowitz of the University of Chicago, suggests that the various motivations shared by newspeople, notably the public service concept, have led to the development of two general models of professionalism. Most journalists, he says, tend to follow one or the other of these models—the "gatekeeper" and the "advocate." Whichever model the journalist chooses as a guide, the choice is likely to result in some conflicts within the news organization.

The "gatekeeper" model, according to Janowitz, emphasizes the journalist's ability "to detect, emphasize, and disseminate that which was important.'' The gatekeeper attempts to report objectively and to keep the reporting of fact separate from the advancement of opinion.

The advocacy journalist, however, ''must be an advocate for those who are denied powerful spokesmen, and he must point out the consequences of the contemporary power imbalance. The search for objective reality yields to a struggle to participate in the socio-political process by supplying knowledge and information.''[6]

These brief summaries perhaps oversimplify Janowitz's careful, detailed analysis. But they do suggest why wholehearted espousal of either model may be a factor in shaping the news, and in generating internal tensions within the newspaper staff or the broadcast news team.

A reporter who sees himself or herself acting in the role of gatekeeper makes decisions at the point at which news is gathered. The gatekeeper expects to exercise autonomy in determining what is ''important'' and thus worth passing on to the public. Responding to Walter Lippmann's definition that ''the function of news is to signalize an event,'' the gatekeeper makes decisions that either signalize or obliterate an event, or specific aspects of an event, so far as entry into the flow of news is concerned.

However, there are others in the newsgathering and -processing chain: city editors or broadcast news directors, copy editors and anchorpersons. Their handling of the news item as it moves along the pipeline may significantly modify or even negate the original gatekeeper's signalizing decisions. Even if all who are in the processing chain follow the gatekeeper model, they may differ widely on such points as news judgment, or the working definition of that impossibly elusive term, *objectivity*. Some conflicts and tests of wills are almost inevitable.

The conflicts are likely to be even more frequent and more intense if the front-line reporters envision themselves in the advocate role. As Janowitz points out, the advocate journalist's ideal is that ''of the lawyer and almost that of the politician''[7]—a journalistic Ralph Nader, in other words.

Many journalists who embrace the advocate model are young and relative newcomers to the field. Their seniors up the line of news processing are likely to be older and more oriented to the gatekeeper and objectivity concepts than to the advocate's concern to provide a voice for unheard elements in society. Thus the advocate's attempts to fulfill that role may routinely be frustrated by the editing (gatekeeping) decisions of editors or producers at other points in the news organization.

Daniel Schorr, long a top-ranking newsman for CBS-TV, told an American University audience that ''it may well be that suppression by one's organization is a greater threat than suppression by the government.'' He said that reporters may have to ''act in defiance of the large news corporations'' in order to do their jobs.[8]

Schorr may have been overdramatizing to make a point, but the point is one with which many working journalists might sympathize. The news is shaped in part by the ongoing internal struggle between those in the field who make the initial decisions as to what will be reported or filmed, and thus become the stuff of the news, and those who later in the news processing and disseminating chain amend or nullify the earlier decisions by ones made at an editor's desk or in a producer's booth.

Much of the time, all the persons working within a given medium have like goals and work together harmoniously. But the conditions that foster differences and conflicts are inherent in the nature of the business. Journalists feel strongly about the significance of their role, and about the obligation of public service that is built into it. When perceptions of the role and the obligation differ among those in the same organization—as, for example, between gatekeepers and advocates—the differences can become lively and heated. And the picture of the world that the news eventually brings to us can be shaded or narrowed significantly by the outcome of the internal jockeying.

Conflicts caused by other kinds of differences can also develop within a news organization and affect the end product.

In section 1 we noted how an overall ownership decision to maximize profits can be a factor in shaping the nature of the news disseminated by a newspaper or broadcast station. Such an overall decision by top ownership must be implemented within the organization, and it is at this point that the consequences are most readily apparent. A newspaper's news staff is held to an absolute minimum, as an example, allowing bare-bones coverage of the essential happenings. But the extra five, ten, or twenty reporters who would make the difference between a minimum level of coverage and the kind of searching, investigative reporting that gets behind surface events and invests the news with real meaning cannot be hired, because that would boost operating budgets and pare profit margins.

The same thing happens on a broadcast network, when economic considerations rule out the allocation of funds and staff power to undertake documentaries that dig deeply into a complex problem. Or when a top newsman, Fred Friendly, resigns as president of CBS News in protest over his network's refusal to preempt some lucrative soap opera time to allow the televising of a crucial Senate foreign relations hearing.

But not all ownership-staff relationships that affect the nature of news are rooted in economics. The personal or political phobias of some strong-minded owners have in the past been forced on news staffs, and as a consequence the news has been variously slanted or misrepresented. In their day, such media barons as the elder William Randolph Hearst, with his powerful chain of metropolitan newspapers, handed down dicta about topics or persons to be banned from the pages of all publications under their control. Robert R. McCormick of the *Chicago Tribune* was of that mold, too. *Tribune* staff members had standing orders to give heavy play to any negative news about the British (one of McCormick's hates) or vivisection.

The corporate era and an increasing sense of public responsibility among media owners have reduced the number of such ownership types on the contemporary scene, but they haven't disappeared. We still have William Loeb, publisher of the *Manchester* (New Hampshire) *Union-Leader,* whose staff members are expected to abet his ultraconservative objectives in the news columns as well as on the editorial page of his paper. And until recently we still had William Paley of the Columbia Broadcasting System. As one network official put it: "CBS is run like Constantinople in the seventh century. No one makes a move without checking with the caliph [Paley]."[9]

In most of the media today, however, the shaping of news by ownership impact on staff members is not likely to be in the form of imperial directives. Nor does it need to be.

Awareness of ownership viewpoints, pet peeves, or sacred cows can seep through a news organization as though by osmosis. Nothing need be too obvious. A story gutted ("for space reasons"); a reporter abruptly pulled off one assignment and sent to another; a mediocre event given unaccountably strong front page play—these are enough in the way of signals to a discerning staff member.

That doesn't mean that staff members always acquiesce in such gentle suasion. Two of my former students have resigned newspaper jobs in protest over the reshaping of their copy to accommodate ownership demands. Another was fired when a vigorous investigative series he was developing for a Southern daily began to come uncomfortably close to a local political figure who was also a good friend of the publisher. Other reporters in situations where ownership policies were resulting in radical alteration of copy refused to allow their by-lines to appear on the stories in contention. Or they invoked Newspaper Guild or some other union intervention to deal with the dispute.

POWER—UP TO A POINT

Disputes inevitably arise because there is a paradox built into the news organization structure. Reporters, by strongly entrenched convention, have autonomy in the newsgathering and newswriting functions. However, the decisions on which stories reporters will cover, and the final editing and processing of the finished copy, are typically handled by persons other than the original newsgatherer. There is reporter power up to a point; then management's hand is felt, perhaps with critical effect.

True enough, on very small papers a reporter may cover a story, write the copy, prepare a headline, and even give the item a slot in the makeup schedule. But the larger the operation, the greater the degree of specialization that will be evident, and the more reduced will be the area of reporter autonomy.

A study by Illinois Professor John W. C. Johnstone revealed that more than three-quarters of responding reporters on papers of all sizes said that they had almost complete freedom in how they wrote stories. Yet only a third of those same respondents claimed that the stories they wrote went into the paper unedited by any other staff members; and the percentage claiming such sweeping autonomy ranged from 55 percent on the smallest papers studied (with 1 to 5 employees) down to only 7 percent on the largest group (more than 200 employees).[10]

This situation can lead to a kind of operational standoff in news coverage. The reporter shapes the story initially by selecting details, quotes, incidents; aspects left out at this point are probably lost forever, so far as finding their way into the news is concerned. Farther down the pipeline, deft pencil work on the copy desk (or, more likely these days, on the console of the video display terminal) can revamp the story to some degree. And, of course, the final placement of the item in the paper or newscast can determine significantly the amount of attention it will get from the ultimate consumer. It is perhaps important to repeat a point noted earlier: on some media operations there is like-thinking commitment all the way up the line; in such situations, the original newsgatherer may be confident that the story will pass through the processing stages without significant modification. But such harmony isn't evident on most newspapers or broadcast news operations.

For example, it is a fact that most newspaper management representatives tend to be more politically conservative than the reporters and other staff members on the same publication. Editorial page endorsements by newspapers have in most elections been overwhelmingly Republican; surveys of the political leanings of rank-and-file staffers indicate that they are almost as emphatically in the Democratic camp.

Even though all concerned may set about their tasks intending impartial coverage, some unconscious slanting is likely, followed usually by management-staff tension. Unflattering photographs of the candidates favored by ownership will be vetoed at the desk even though, somehow, the photographer happened that day to catch only unflattering angles and poses. A cartoonist's rough will be rejected because management thinks it hits unfairly at the paper's candidate. Stories showing the management choice in a favorable light will get generous front page space, while the opponent's coverage is tucked inside (though the number of column inches of space allocated to each may be scrupulously equalized).

Some observers of the press have suggested that the liberal leanings of the working journalists and the conservative bent of most publishers and owners fortunately offset each other, with the result a relatively balanced blend of political news coverage. That is perhaps a too simplified conclusion.

As a footnote to the discussion of conflicts within the media, we might acknowledge various isolated developments stemming from these tensions.

One has been the development of the concept of ''reporter power'' and the so-called revolt in the newsroom. Union chapters or other organizations of reporters have sought to obtain concessions from management that would give rank-and-file staff members a voice in policy decisions. (In this they have taken a leaf from experiments in other countries, particularly on *Le Monde* in Paris, where to varying degrees staff members have won participation in management.) The result, in some newsrooms, has been the organization of reporters' committees that investigate conflicts, consult with management, and help enhance reporter autonomy whenever possible. One publisher, John McCormally of the *Burlington* (Iowa) *Hawkeye*, voluntarily established a system whereby his staff members elect the paper's managing editor.

The reporter revolt has not yet manifested itself generally, however. An inhibiting factor has been the journalistic job market, which in recent years has given employers the edge. There are, after all, only about 70,000 full-time journalists in all the United States news media.[11] And in recent years there have been as many as 64,000 students in journalism schools and departments at one time. Not all of these students have been heading toward the 70,000 news and editorial positions, to be sure; many are going into advertising, public relations, or teaching. Nonetheless, the numbers of news-editorial graduates being produced have been greater than the job market could absorb. That has led to a situation that has understandably dampened the militancy of the reporter power movement.

Some newspapers are actually owned by the employees (the *Milwaukee Journal*) or were until recently (the *Kansas City Star*), but this situation typically came about through the actions of publishers who set up the arrangement in their wills. It is revealing that on such employee-owned papers there is a distinct management factor (even though the board of directors may be named by the stockholding employees) and much the same sorts of tensions that are found on conventionally structured publications.

One outgrowth of the tensions within news media has been the appearance of media reviews in various cities. Such reviews are typically staffed by local journalists, and their mission is to criticize the performance of the media for which the staff members work. We'll discuss these reviews later in greater detail.

SUMMARY

We have inventoried the motivations that draw persons into the field of journalism. These motivations are important to understand if we want to know how and why the news is shaped before it is presented to us through the media channels.

We have also looked into the tensions, the pressures and counterpressures, and the organizational characteristics of the media, all of which are important influences on the shape of the news we get. They are literally the forces that make the media tick.

We need next to turn our attention to relationships between the media and those agencies and individuals elsewhere in society who are the sources of news. In some instances we'll be looking at these relationships in general, institutional terms, as between medium and source. In other cases we'll be exploring the ramifications of the relationship of individual journalists with specific news sources.

We'll begin by looking at relationships—both institutional and individual—involving the media and the various branches of government. For government, at all levels, represents the single biggest news beat for all of journalism, and one of the most complex and difficult to cover.

5
The Biggest Beat: Government

I. F. Stone, the irascible, pungent editor for many years of a weekly news and opinion letter from Washington, once observed that "every government is run by liars and nothing they say should be believed."[12] Stone's observation epitomizes in the extreme a notion widely held by journalists in all media: that the natural relationship between newspeople and government officials at all levels is adversarial.

The First Amendment specifically prohibits government from interfering with the freedom of the press. Through the years, journalists have interpreted this prohibition to mean that the press has been designated the public's agent to watch over the activities of government. It is manifestly impossible, so the reasoning goes, for all members of the public to keep a wary eye on the performance of those who are elected or appointed to administer the public's business. Thus the press acts as proxy for the people, maintaining a vigilant watch on officialdom and sounding the alarm when malfeasance, misfeasance, or extracurricular hanky-panky is discovered.

The concept of the adversary relationship has reinforced the notion of the press as the "fourth branch of government," an adjunct to the system of checks and balances that the Constitution-makers fashioned in the three-branch federal structure. The Constitution, of course, says nothing about the press as a fourth branch, or even as a watchdog on behalf of the public; the adversary concept has evolved by extension of the First Amendment language, fostered by journalists, political scientists, and logic.

Government officials are entrusted with vast power over the lives and fortunes of the American people. With that power come temptations that at least some government officials cannot resist. What agency, if not the press, will blow the whistle on erring servants who succumb to temptation and abuse the power temporarily entrusted to them?

Also, even the best-intentioned politician must confront the reality of election day, when his or her future will again be in the hands of the voters. There is an irresistible tendency for anyone in that situation to put the best foot forward and tuck the other one as far out of sight as possible. The press sees its duty as keeping both feet of political leaders in public view so that the voters' ballot box decision will be informed.

Thus government and the news media, by their nature, fall into an adversary relationship. When the next coup or revolution takes place somewhere in the world, watch what happens. The first action of the new regime will likely be to clamp down on the press, to shut off the flow of news until it can be molded to suit the objectives of those who have taken power. It has happened with the advent of Fascist or Communist dictatorships in Germany, Italy, Russia, and China, and more recently in Chile, Argentina, India, Vietnam, Thailand, and many other nations where freedom went into eclipse.

Even in nations that are not authoritarian, there is unwillingness to accept the concepts of media freedom and the adversary relationship. The Third World nations, for example, have advanced a "development theory" of the press: while a new nation is struggling to establish itself economically and stabilize itself politically, the press should cooperate in these efforts. Only news that furthers the objectives of development (that is, government policies) should be disseminated; "negative" news should be suppressed. In late 1976, representatives of 85 nonaligned nations attending a conference in Sri Lanka endorsed the establishment of a Third World news agency that would supplant free press agencies and expand the "development theory" of the press to whole regions of the globe.[13]

The history of the United States is studded with episodes that suggest the persistence and inevitability of the adversarial press-government relationship.

The alien and sedition laws of the early nineteenth century represented an effort by both executive and legislative branches of government of that era to cripple the freedom of the press. In our time, when the CBS network aired a documentary, "The Selling of the Pentagon," members of Congress aroused by the show's critical portrayal of government propaganda activities sought to wield the contempt power of Congress to force the network to yield up reporters' notes and discarded film footage for a congressional committee's scrutiny. That attempt, and a later one by another committee to force correspondent Daniel Schorr to reveal confidential sources, both failed when the legislators backed off in the final showdown. But even though they failed, the attempts undoubtedly led to greater caution on the part of broadcasters in treating later controversial topics and thus were in part successful.

Presidents from Washington to Carter have fumed about the press. Even Thomas Jefferson, one of the earliest, most eloquent supporters of the free press, later turned against the newspapers and berated them as deceitful. Some chief executives have gone beyond talk, as did Richard Nixon when a handful of newspapers printed excerpts of the secret Pentagon Papers that revealed how the nation had become embroiled in the Vietnam war. The executive branch threw its whole might into the fight to prevent publication of the papers, but failed thanks to a narrow Supreme Court decision.

Even the courts have shared to some degree in the adversary syndrome, sending journalists to jail for refusing to violate the confidentiality of sources, or issuing gag orders to prevent complete coverage of trials.

In moments of quiet reason, most government officials acknowledge the importance of the watchdog role of the press. Legislatures in nearly half the states have enacted shield laws to help the news media protect the anonymity of news sources. And every state constitution affords to the press the same freedom from government interference embodied in the First Amendment. Yet when push comes to shove, journalists and politicians know how they stand in relation to each other. Both have power, with sharply differing objectives in its use. Both have missions, sometimes similar but more often opposed.

Perhaps at no time have the various aspects of the press-government relationship come into clearer or more dramatic focus than during the presidential administration of Richard Nixon, 1969 to 1974.

THE PRESS AND THE NIXON YEARS

The period between Nixon's election in 1968 through the day of his resignation in 1974 is a useful setting in which to examine the press-government relationship and how it shapes the nature of the news we read, watch, and hear. Later we'll look at counterpart situations at the other levels of government, less dramatic but nonetheless important to us as consumers of media products.

Many books have been written about what happened, stage by stage, from that first Nixon victory to the Watergate unraveling. We can only touch on those developments that bear upon the subject under discussion in this chapter.

Early in his career Richard Nixon developed a sharp adversary relationship with the press. He blamed the media in large part for his loss of the presidential election of 1960, and he let his bitterness show in his celebrated tirade against the press in 1962, after his defeat in the California gubernatorial race ("You won't have Richard Nixon to kick around any more"). Yet after his carefully crafted comeback and narrow win over Hubert Humphrey in 1968, President Nixon began to demonstrate that he had come to understand the adversary relationship well enough to exploit and manipulate it masterfully.

Of all political figures, a president has maximum leverage in his relationships with the news media. He can command newspaper space or broadcast time whenever he chooses to hold a press conference or report to the nation on a matter of significance.

In a press conference setting, a president can to a considerable degree control the flow of news emanating from the interchange. He recognizes the next questioner amid the insistent clamor of "Mr. President!" He knows which correspondents are likely to raise safe issues and pose the sort of questions to which an ambiguous response can be made. Since a televised press conference provides unusual visibility for a journalist, it is not difficult for a skillful presidential press secretary to plant questions with compliant correspondents eager to be heard and seen in so momentous a role.

Nixon used the press conference sparingly but effectively during his first administration. He also caused to be mounted a deliberate and concerted campaign to undermine public confidence in the press and to put journalism on the defensive. His vice president attacked the "unelected elite" who dominated the news, slashing at broadcasters, newspapers, and newsmagazines alike as belonging to an establishment conspiracy to slant the news. The White House communications director voiced veiled but significant threats against the broadcast media. Administration officials cultivated the few friendly media representatives, feeding them exclusive tips and interviews while freezing out the hostiles.

It was, overall, a remarkably successful performance. Toward the end of the first Nixon administration the national press was obviously on the defensive, unable to join battle with a news source enveloped in the built-in protections of the presidency, and clearly suffering a drain of public confidence under the orchestrated attack mounted by the administration. Some observers have concluded that the failure of most of the Washington-based press to uncover the full extent of Watergate in the very early stages was directly attributable to the timidity and demoralization to which the media had been reduced by the administration offensive.

Of course, Nixon was not the first chief executive to manipulate the news media for his own ends, nor the first to attempt to intimidate them.

Franklin D. Roosevelt used radio adroitly, by means of his fireside chats, to reach the people directly. He also knew how to wield the leverage of the presidency to make news, to keep himself and his activities on the front page and thus offset the almost unanimous editorial page opposition of the newspapers. John F. Kennedy used the televised press conference to great effect, his wit and style charming both correspondents and viewing public. And Lyndon B. Johnson repeatedly threatened and scolded newspapers and broadcast media when they failed to portray the news as he saw it, in Vietnam and at home. He also cultivated certain correspondents, drew them into the heady White House circle, and in effect co-opted them and extracted their watchdog fangs.

Yet none of Nixon's predecessors succeeded in the press-government relationship as dramatically as did Nixon, up to the fateful days of Watergate. And his accomplishments were against formidable odds. Virtually no member of the working press in Washington or elsewhere had much use or respect for

Nixon. The attitude went back to Nixon's days in the House of Representatives and the Senate, through his vice presidential years and his first campaign for the presidency, when the *Washington Post*'s Herblock caricatured him in vicious, memorable terms. As one correspondent put it, talking for himself and his colleagues: "Nixon's supporters are largely right about us—we do not like their man and we never have. . . ."[14]

Still, in the face of this attitude by the print and broadcast journalists who covered him, Nixon had managed by the beginning of his campaign for a second term to manipulate, undermine, and intimidate the media to the extent that he could campaign entirely on his own terms and simultaneously keep the Watergate affair bottled up until after his landslide victory was part of American political history. The adversary relationship that normally protects the public interest from the machinations of politicians and the abuse of public trust had been effectively neutralized.

It was not only Nixon's handling of the adversary relationship that had brought about this state of affairs. Two other factors, also involving media relationships with news sources, had played a part: the "official sources syndrome" and the "inner circle" mentality that chronically afflicts newsgathering in Washington.

OFFICIAL SOURCES
AND THE INNER CIRCLE

The official sources syndrome is the tendency of many reporters to rely excessively on news that comes to them from the agencies and individuals who are perceived as spokespersons for their constituencies or their causes. Newsgathering is often a tedious, drawn-out process of probing, questioning, and digging; the reporter must overcome buck-passing, evasiveness, "no-comments," and the constant pressure of deadlines. In the circumstances it is not surprising that many reporters come to lean on dependable, accessible founts of news—press secretaries for high officials, department handouts with the "news" already predigested and polished (and usually slanted, a trifle or a lot), and visible spokespersons for government agencies, the congressional chairmen and the chief lobbyists for powerful interest groups. Reporters can make the rounds of the official sources, confident that all that is necessary is to turn the spigot and the news will flow.

There is a critical flaw in overdependence on official sources. Those who speak for an official or an agency are almost automatically and inevitably self-serving; they may provide a truthful enough version of the news, but it is rarely a *complete* version. Moreover, for some kinds of news there are no convenient spokespersons, no official sources. Uncovering such kinds of news may require hard work and much time.

Thus some Washington newsgatherers fall into the habit of making the familiar rounds, garnering the handouts, and compiling the views of the official representatives—and failing to obtain balancing versions and views from unorganized but important segments of society. One long-time Washington correspondent, Clark Mollenhoff of the *Des Moines Register* and *Tribune*, contends that only a handful of reporters at the nation's capital really cover the news; the rest, he says, do their reporting on the basis of agency handouts and Press Club gossip.

During the first stages of Watergate the official sources syndrome, coupled with the caution that had been bred in the press by the administration's successful campaign to undermine public confidence in the media, led many reporters to accept on their face the disclaimers from the White House and the Committee to Re-Elect the President. Watergate was dismissed as a "third-rate burglary," a bungling attempt by underlings, with little or no news value. The majority of the correspondents turned to other, more obviously newsworthy events.

The "inner circle" phenomenon of Washington coverage also contributed to the situation. Reporters assigned by a paper, network, or magazine to the Washington beat soon discover that their value to the home office increases as they acquire access to exclusive or semi-exclusive pipelines. After all, the wire services (AP, UPI, *New York Times*, and others) do the vacuum-cleaner job of checking all pending legislation, happenings on the floor of the House or Senate, and White House briefings or news conferences. The special correspondent in Washington becomes worth his or her salt only by establishing relationships that lead to news leaks and tips not swept up in the wire service coverage. If a correspondent never develops such pipelines, the Washington assignment may be a brief one.

However, establishing sources, finding an "inner circle" from which to operate, is not so difficult as one might assume. There are in Washington hundreds of persons—members of Congress, executive branch officials, even high federal judges—who are very much aware of the importance of the media to their careers. Cabinet officers, powerful Senate or House leaders, agency heads—virtually all gradually assemble small groups of journalists with whom they meet more or less regularly on an informal basis, at a monthly dinner, to "strike a blow for liberty" in the Speaker's back office, or around a luncheon table at some correspondent's home. Here, off the record, the government official passes on news tips, floats trial balloons, tries out ideas, or sets in motion an act of vengeance on some rival. The relationship is interdependent, of course: the correspondents obtain exclusive information from "sources close to . . ." while the official gets in some propaganda licks or settles old scores.

The symbiotic nature of the relationship is basically invidious so far as the reportorial function is concerned. True, some news that wouldn't otherwise surface does get out. But debts also pile up. A reporter is unlikely to endanger an "inner circle" relationship by filing a story exposing or reflecting on his choice pipeline source. Inner circle arrangements lead to a fusing of the interests of the reporters and the news sources, to the extent that the shape of the news we get may be warped significantly without our ever realizing it.

For example, that some members of Congress were heavy drinkers—even to the point of becoming incompetent in their jobs—was common knowledge at the bar of the Washington Press Club for years, but the facts were never printed until a few highly placed figures tangled with the Washington police and thus automatically made the news via the municipal court. Washington correspondents had indulgently ignored the stories until forced by events to mention them, because the figures involved were news sources too invaluable to alienate.

This inner ring attitude on the part of many newspeople in Washington contributed to the situation that had developed by the end of Richard Nixon's first administration. It wasn't that the President or his chief aides cultivated such an intimate circle of correspondents; far from it. Their strategy was attack. But plenty of other administration and congressional figures did maintain collections of media chums, and they could help to send the reporters on other trails, away from Watergate. One way or another, the adversary relationship between press and government had been so vitiated by 1972 that it failed to function in the expected way.

In fact, it was the dogged effort of two low-level *Washington Post* reporters that finally uncovered the iceberg of Watergate and led to the downfall of a president. Bob Woodward and Carl Bernstein were not members of any inner circle, nor were they conversant with official sources. They were not even capitol correspondents, but members of the metropolitan staff of the newspaper, usually assigned to purely local stories.

They discovered the Watergate story because it began as a police blotter episode; they followed it out, step by slow step, not by going the rounds of official spokespersons or tapping friendly pipelines, but by plugging away in the classic newsgathering sense. At the outset they were virtually alone in their effort; for reasons we mentioned above, most other reporters and correspondents had transferred their attention elsewhere: to the developing campaign, to the high drama of Senator Thomas Eagleton's departure from the McGovern ticket, and to soothing news releases from official sources.

As the dimensions of the story became more apparent to Woodward and Bernstein, they indulged—by their own admission—in practices that ethical journalists normally would shun: prying information from grand jurors, employing deception and entrapment, playing upon intragovernment enmities. Woodward and Bernstein felt justified in fighting fire with fire, convinced as they were that they were pitted against the massive weight of an entire administration riddled with corruption.

The two reporters fully embraced the adversary concept, and in the end they saw themselves and the concept both triumphant. Although at the outset their labor was lonely and risky, they had plenty of company later, when the conspiracy began to fall apart. Then their colleagues in all media belatedly took up the adversary role, and with a vengenace. What James Reston has called "the artillery of the press" quickly found the range and began pouring an unending and punishing fire on the target.

CLOSING IN FOR THE KILL

In their eagerness to catch up with the exploits of Woodward and Bernstein, and perhaps also in search of revenge for the intimidation of the earlier Nixon years, the press as a whole indulged in an excess of vituperative pursuit that somewhat tarnished the solid achievement of the Watergate disclosures. The display of overkill was unseemly in the judgment of some observers and ominous in the eyes of others.

One British correspondent, for example, exulted in these terms after watching Nixon's televised resignation speech:

> As we saw—for, I hoped, the last time—that nasty, snarling little withdrawal of lip from teeth which passed for a Nixon smile, I felt that the only appropriate and more or less creditable exit for him would be suicide.[15]

Somewhat later Irving Kristol, a frequent critic of the press, evaluated this and like excesses:

> . . . "power," for the media, means the power to discredit and destroy—it is through such successes that they acquire visible signs of grace. After Watergate, the media are in a state of mind that can only be described as manic. They feverishly seek new victims, prominent ones if possible, obscure ones if necessary. There is the smell of blood in the air, and of fire and brimstone, too.[16]

The resurgence of the adversary concept carried over into the 1976 presidential campaign and led some journalists to leap at every morsel of gossip or hint of scandal in the hope of tipping over another iceberg and winning the kind of national fame and fortune that had come to the two *Post* reporters. Woodward and Bernstein contributed to the mood of the press with their second book, *The Final Days,* which was concerned less with recounting how their reportage uncovered Watergate than with probing the personalities of the principal actors in the national tragedy, indulging in sometimes tasteless and thinly substantiated revelations about the fallen great and those close to them.

Thus the Nixon presidential era provides a textbook review of the functioning of the adversary concept of press-government relationships. At one period, weakened by a studied, well-executed government offensive, the concept had virtually faded from the scene; later it was revived so vigorously and pressed so ruthlessly that it caused at least some members of the public and some analysts of the press to become alarmed at the implications of the unleashed power of the press.

Before we end this discussion of the adversary relationship and its varying expression during the Nixon years, two aspects of press coverage of the Watergate episode deserve detailed examination. One is Woodward and Bernstein's heavy reliance upon anonymous news sources as they worked through their painstaking revelation of the conspiracy's extent.

It must be acknowledged that the two reporters had little choice. The informants they were able to reach were embedded in the government bureaucracy; it would have been fatal to their careers to come forward as public witnesses against their powerful superiors. So the *Post* reporters did the best they could to verify the tips or admissions they obtained from the faceless accusers, requiring substantiation from several quarters before accepting a particular revelation as likely to be authentic. They maintained a solid batting average in the process; very few of their reports were later shown to be unsupported by hard evidence.

But grave dangers are inherent in reliance upon anonymous sources. This was underlined in the post-Watergate period, when journalists eager to emulate the success of the *Post* duo began to flood the newspapers and airwaves with stories fed to them by secret sources—only to find later that the information was distorted or even wholly fabricated. Woodward and Bernstein themselves came under criticism for *The Final Days*, which depicted conversations and meetings in which only two persons were involved. Since the reporters themselves had not talked with either of the two, they were obviously basing their story on second- or third-hand accounts, which any sound reporter knows enough to discount as likely to have been embellished at each successive retelling. As press analyst Edward Jay Epstein observes of a quote attributed to Secretary of State Henry Kissinger in *The Final Days:*

> The authors claim they would have to have heard the quote from at least two individuals, which attests not to the provenance of the quote but [to] the fact that it has been circulating in certain circles. Such data, of course, cannot be logically distinguished from gossip.[17]

In the past, reporters rarely made use of anonymous sources, since the source of an item of information is itself part of the news and ought under ordinary circumstances to be made available to the public. But in the aftermath of Watergate the incidence of news stories based on reports from unnamed sources has risen disturbingly, particularly in major dailies. A study commissioned by the American Newspaper Publishers Association Foundation and conducted by Professor Hugh Culbertson of Ohio University showed that in the *New York Times* and *Washington Post* 54 percent of all ''straight news'' stories (that is, excluding sports, theater, opinion, weather) were based entirely or in part on one or more unnamed sources; the percentage for four other metropolitan newspapers was 36 percent; and for six small Ohio dailies, 30 percent.[18] These findings ought to concern any consumer of the news media who would like to know from whom the news comes, so that the reliability of the source may be weighed along with the news item itself.

There are indeed situations in which it is appropriate and even essential for reporters to base news stories on unnamed sources; Watergate was one of these, as are news breaks volunteered by subordinates able to provide evidence of wrongdoing by their superiors. The only way the reporter can investigate such stories is by promising anonymity to the informer. And if the story is important to the public interest, that is the course the reporter feels obliged to take, even if it carries risk of contempt charges from a judge.

But such situations do not arise daily, or even once a month for most reporters on most papers. The incidence of reliance on faceless accusers revealed by the Culbertson study is not consistent with sound journalism. Moreover, it constitutes an open invitation to the public to discount the credibility of the media that so frequently call upon their readers to accept on faith that ''sources close to . . .'' or ''spokesmen for . . .'' truly exist and actually did say the things they are quoted as having said.

"INSTINCT FOR THE JUGULAR"

A second aspect of the role of the press in the Watergate and post-Watergate eras is the spirit of hot pursuit that animated many journalists then, and continues to some extent to this day. Irving Kristol called it a ''manic'' state of mind into which the media had fallen. Charles Seib, ombudsman of the *Washington Post,* worried about the way that ''the relentless press pursues its search for misbehavior, great and small . . .'' and in the process displays ''an aggravated instinct for the jugular. . . .'' And John R. (Reg) Murphy, editor and publisher of the San Francisco *Examiner*, observed that ''there are far too many reporters who have smelled the blood in the water and have gone after any weaknesses they can find.''

Among the weaknesses found and trumpeted to the world:

Joan Kennedy (wife of Senator Edward Kennedy) spent a week at a center for treatment of alcoholics.
Senator Hugh Scott's daughter (age 41) was arrested on a minor drug charge.

Charles Abourezk, son of South Dakota Senator James Abourezk, was living on food stamps.

A cousin of former President Richard Nixon was on welfare, and another had gone bankrupt.

The late John F. Kennedy may have had sexual relationships with several women while president.

During the 1976 presidential campaign hardly a week went by without some headline-grabbing revelation by columnist Jack Anderson, Woodward and Bernstein, or one of their emulators. In a few cases the stories turned out to have substance; in many others they were shown to be utterly groundless, cheap shots by journalists with restless trigger fingers and ambitions for fame in a hurry.

Seib of the *Post* deplored his paper's use of the Abourezk item as "the urge to expose gone wild." H. L. Stevenson, head of United Press International, has commented that turning gossip into fact is a '70s phenomenon, but he was skeptical that this would, in the long run, keep people informed.[19] He had a right to be skeptical—and so has the public when the media appear to be engaged in a wholesale effort to shape the news to serve frivolous or unworthy ends.

Watergate demonstrated the power of the news media. That demonstration impressed the public and officialdom alike, but it also generated some concerns. If there is continuing evidence that the awesome leverage of the media is being used in unjustifiable ways not related to public service or social responsibility, it is conceivable that an effort could be mounted to impose curbs upon the press, despite the First Amendment. As columnist Joseph Kraft has warned, "Our privileges are fragile; there is nothing automatic about freedom of the press. . . ."[20] Former Senator William Fulbright, a frequent and outspoken defender of the media, was similarly solemn:

> A free society can remain free only as long as its citizens exercise restraint in the practice of their freedom. This principle applies with special force to the press, because of its power and because of its necessary immunity from virtually every form of restraint except self-restraint. . . .[21]

Such warnings were echoed a few years later during an episode involving press coverage reminiscent of some phases of the Watergate affair. In 1977 President Carter's director of the Office of Management and Budget, Bert Lance, came under press scrutiny when some of his activities as a Georgia banker were shown to be unusual, if not irregular. After investigation by several government agencies, during which the media kept the spotlight of coverage relentlessly on Lance and his background, the OMB director resigned his post.

Some of Lance's supporters blamed the press. Representative John J. Flynt of Georgia complained that "Bert Lance was charged, tried and convicted by a lynch mob. . . ." Another Georgian, Senator Sam Nunn, decried "this media festival which has been conducted for so long at the expense of one man's honor and reputation." At least one journalist appeared to be in partial agreement. Columnist George F. Will of *Newsweek* observed that "any town full of journalists and politicians will be fond of blood sports. Washington hasn't had a good kill for a while, and Lance is a large, slow stag. . . ."

Most journalists, however, denied that press coverage of the Lance case involved the kinds of excesses evident during some stages of Watergate and its aftermath. Columnist Nick Thimmesch probably spoke for many of his colleagues when he wrote: "Bert Lance was not victimized by the press. He was a legitimate subject of press curiosity, then inquiry, followed by development of facts which skinned him."

STATEHOUSE AND CITY HALL

The several press-government relationships that we have examined in detail as they are manifested in the nation's capital are also evident at other levels of government. The relationships—particularly the adversary relationship—may be less intense than on the Washington scene and less likely to engender dramatic controversy, but most of the same basic elements are present.

At the local level, the mayor and the city hall reporters may not often think of themselves in adversarial terms. They are all members of the same community; goals of civic betterment may often coincide; there may be personal relationships of long standing. To be sure, there are notable exceptions: Mayor Frank Rizzo of Philadelphia, former Mayor Richard Daley of Chicago, and Mayor Frank Fasi of Honolulu maintained drawn-out, bitterly antagonistic feuds with the media of their respective communities. But in the typical middle-sized or small community, the adversary relationship is muted much of the time.

It is also true that local coverage may involve much less reliance on anonymous sources than is the case in Washington. Local readers or viewers would be impatient with the "sources close to . . ." approach in the small-scale setting of community administration.

Actually, the problems inherent in press-government relationships at state and local levels are more likely to stem from a withering of the adversary relationship than from overemphasis on it. The police beat reporter, for example, must cultivate close ties with the sergeants and desk officers who make available information from the police blotter. (In most communities police records are not automatically public and open to the press; only through the cooperation of the police can reporters obtain access to these records.) Once this cooperative relationship has been established, the reporter may naturally be loath to disrupt it by reporting something that reflects unfavorably on the police. It is revealing that a city editor who has a tip on police corruption almost invariably assigns to the story a reporter who is not ordinarily on the police beat and thus has no friendly relationships to cloud his perception as he launches an investigation.

Journalists who regularly cover city hall run the risk of identifying with the objectives of the mayor or city manager, just as a sports writer becomes at least to some degree a rooter for the teams he or she regularly covers.

There are similar problems on the state level. Regulars on the state capitol beat develop first-name friendships with the governor, or the state senate president, or agency heads. Moreover, in every state reporters who cover state government activities are provided with free office space, frequently spacious and expansively equipped. (Four states charge rent; in the other forty-six the office space is on the house—the statehouse that is.)[22]

In such circumstances it is not difficult to understand that the adversary relationship might not be so clear-cut as it often is on the national scene. This is not to say that state and local government reporters are typically pushovers. Pulitzer Prize annals and the rosters of other awards are crowded with recognition of the part played by journalists in uncovering corruption and scandal in state and local government. But the level of tension in the adversary relationship tends to be lower, the smaller the arena and the closer the contact between the representatives of government and those of the press.

SUMMARY

We have been scrutinizing the relationships between reporters and government news sources, noting the purpose, the successes, and the failures of the adversary relationship that frequently characterizes the reporter-source interchange at various levels of government.

The relationship is most dramatic in Washington, where much of the nation's business is done and the power stakes are highest. But it exists at all levels of government, typically with diminishing intensity as the size of the government unit under consideration decreases.

We have seen the interdependence of reporters and government sources, a factor that opposes the adversary concept; this interdependence is evident in the "official sources syndrome" and the "inner circle" mentality, both of which characterize reporter-source relationships at all government levels and both of which can result in a watering down or a reshaping of the news without the ultimate consumer being aware of the alterations that have taken place.

Government is indeed the biggest beat for most media; a substantial part of each day's news budget consists of items emanating from the activities of government officials or agencies at national, state, and local levels.

Yet there are innumerable other beats, and other kinds of ties between reporters and sources that help determine the picture of the world that the media limn for us. We'll look next at some of those other beats, and at special kinds of relationships and problems that affect the ways in which the media perform the tasks we expect of them.

6
Other Sources, Other Problems

Virtually anyone or anything can be or become a news source. Events happen each day by the billions, literally. Very few of them come to the attention of the newsgathering and -disseminating media, sometimes by direct observation but more often through some news source as intermediary. The news source may be an agency fixed in position and regularly functioning as a spigot for news (the city manager's press aide, the desk sergeant at the state police bureau, the White House news secretary). Or it may be an individual citizen thrust momentarily from obscurity into the media spotlight because she or he has witnessed an accident, committed a crime, won a Nobel Prize or a beauty contest.

It would require many books to catalog all of the types of news sources and explore their relationships with newsgatherers. In chapter 5 we examined a few such types, all somehow related to government. In this chapter we'll look at some others. It will not, of course, be an exhaustive inventory; that would be beyond the scope of this text.

Let's turn first to what can be one of the most productive beats other than government: business and industry. What can be said about the relationships between newsgatherers and news sources in this vast sector of society? What kinds of interplay determine what news we learn from the media? What should we, as consumers, bear in mind about how the activities of business and industry are presented to us through various news channels?

Earlier we touched on one form in which news of business and industry finds its way to the media—the news release. News releases come to newspapers, magazines, and broadcast media in all shapes, sizes, and degrees of sophistication. They range from a single dittoed sheet announcing the appointment of a new vice president for marketing to a five-minute minidocumentary film for use on TV—full color, superbly and expensively produced, built around a plausible news situation, and containing perhaps only a fleeting scene designed to further the interests of the company that had the release produced.

The newsgatherer who is the target of the various forms of news releases ideally should scan them warily. There is often legitimate news in such releases. There is also, almost always, some puffery carefully interwoven with the news so that it is difficult to separate the two; the originator hopes, of course, that the reporter, editor, or producer won't take that trouble, but will let the whole package go on through the pipeline to the news columns or the nightly newscast and thus give the PR client some valued exposure.

An experienced hand on a newspaper copy desk can trim away the puff and leave the bare bones of news with as skillful a touch as that of a meat cutter. It is more difficult to strip down a well-made film news release.

The relationship between the print or broadcast journalist and the public relations representative of industry or business is not comparable to the adversary relationship characteristic of government news sources and reporters. But there should be a wary distance, and a recognition that the two serve very different interests.

The reporter and the PR agent are interdependent, often in the same way that a government spokesperson and a Washington reporter may be interdependent. The public relations office is typically the "official spokesman" for much of business and industry, and the chief avenue of approach for the reporter. But the public relations office hopes to have the most favorable possible impression of the client conveyed to the public; the reporter wants as accurate and complete an impression as possible for transmission to the readers or viewers. Their objectives overlap in part—but only in part. That is a crucial distinction.

Proponents of the public relations industry sometimes argue that journalists couldn't do their jobs without the assistance provided by PR people; that there are too few reporters to cover unaided all the various sorts of news that originate in the form of press releases, press conferences, or interviews arranged by public relations offices. There certainly is practical evidence to buttress this claim. One press observer and critic, Ben Bagdikian, estimates that up to 60 percent of the news content of a daily newspaper can be traced to press releases or some other news-originating actions by a public relations office representing a business, a unit of government, an educational institution, or a civic group.

In the circumstances, it is important to the ultimate consumer of the news media product how vigilantly reporters and editors ply their gatekeeper trade, sifting genuine news out of self-serving puffery. That vigilance is affected by various factors, one of which may be relative knowledge and expertise.

Most public relations persons have background in the various media, or at least understand them thoroughly. They have been reporters, editors, or producers themselves; they know how the media tick, where the decision-making points are located, and what craft conditions influence news handling. They are thus in a position to plan releases to coincide with deadlines, and to write those releases with such polish that the copy desk editor will be tempted to railroad the material (send it on through the pipeline without alteration).

Moreover, so far as the business beat is concerned, public relations persons are likely to be better informed about their client companies or industries than are the journalists assigned to this beat. On almost any news staff, print or broadcast, there are likely to be many more writers and editors who are genuinely knowledgeable about government, say, or sports, than there are experts on business, finance, and economics. To be sure, the staffs of the *Wall Street Journal, Business Week,* and *Forbes* include some certified experts on the business beat (although even on such publications there may be a few economic near-illiterates). But on media of general circulation or appeal the well grounded, seriously committed business newswriter is rare.

Covering news of business, industry, and finance is typically not exciting. Stockholders' meetings, corporation quarterly reports, and announcements of personnel changes do not match in drama or interest the events on other beats. Neophyte journalists rarely come equipped with much background in economics and business. Some make the effort to acquire it, but not many. Editors, broadcasters, and media observers alike will agree that on most general media the news of the business beat is less expertly and less perceptively covered than is the case with almost any other sector of the news.

Thus the reporter-source relationship on this beat often finds a relatively uninformed and unenthusiastic journalist dealing with a public relations representative wise in the ways of the media and fully aware of the strong and weak spots in the client company's current situation. It may be a mismatch that results in poor service to the news-consuming public.

FREEBIES—A HARDY BREED

In most of the specialized news areas related to business and industry, news sources or their agents use other approaches besides the news release in an attempt to ensure that journalists will emphasize the good rather than the bad in their coverage.

Food writers and editors for newspapers or broadcast outlets receive numerous invitations each year to attend bake-off competitions sponsored by a cake flour manufacturer, or chicken-cooking contests sponsored by poultry growers. The food writers are offered free transportation, housing, and entertainment as an inducement to attend such affairs. The hope—often realized—of the public relations people who plan such events is that the writers will return to their media and write or say favorable things about cakes or chickens.

Comparable junkets are regularly available for travel writers for newspapers or magazines. They are whisked to exotic resorts, given VIP treatment, and returned tanned and glowing to home base, there (the PR people hope) to extol the pleasures of Waikiki or Rio's beaches.

Many media managers have recently become more strait-laced about such thinly veiled attempts at media bribery (termed "freebies" among journalists). Codes of ethics have been adopted by such groups as the Associated Press Managing Editors Association and the Newspaper Food Writers and Editors Association. These codes supplement the long-established credos of such major journalistic organizations as the American Society of Newspaper Editors and the Society of Professional Journalists, Sigma Delta Chi, both of which condemn freebies specifically. There has been some housecleaning, particularly during the 1970s, but freebies are as hardy as cockroaches and they keep showing up. There are still soft spots, as I noted in a recent book devoted entirely to media ethics, in such areas as:

The real estate sections of newspapers, in which thinly disguised puff stories about local real estate developments are used, as one editor put it, as "shinplaster to keep the ads from bumping."

The fashion reporting scene, in newspapers, magazines, and broadcasting, where the dress-designing firms pay the expenses of reporters coming to New York or Paris to cover the new openings, and where the leading press agent for the fashion industry, Eleanor Lambert, can publicly boast: "I own every fashion editor in America."

The numerous contests and awards offered each year by various commercial or other special-interest groups as inducement to reporters to crank out stories that will put their organizations or products in the public eye. (Examples: the Cigar Institute award for the best photograph of a prominent news figure puffing on a cigar; the American Furniture Mart Awards for reporting on home furnishings; the American Meat Institute awards for reporting about foods.)[23]

The freebie concept, whether it involves nothing more than a few passes to a ball game or something as lavish as a week's trip to Rome to cover a movie premiere, represents an effort to subvert the newsgathering and -disseminating media and shape the news to serve the ends of various special interests. Freebies are not unique to the business and industry sector of the news scene, to be sure; in one form or another they tend to crop up in all kinds of reporter-source relationships. But for various reasons they are more pervasive and persistent in the field of reporting news about business and industry than virtually anywhere else.

This is particularly unfortunate for the consumer of news. Virtually all of us have a stake in what is going on in business, industry, and the management of finance. Half the families in the country include persons who are stockholders in industry; millions of other individuals have an indirect involvement in the stock market because they belong to unions or work for companies whose vast pension funds are invested in equities. And all of us are consumers of the products and services of business and industry and thus need to know as much as possible about the performance of companies, the reliability of products, and the trends in fiscal and economic affairs. Yet for decades the news of business and industry has come in large measure from reporters and editors not thoroughly grounded in the subject matter; and the nature of that news has been shaped at least in part by the deft manipulation of skilled public relations persons.

Happily, the situation has been improving. Better equipped reporters are joining news staffs; national correspondents such as NBC's Irving R. Levine have become knowing specialists; newsmagazines have recruited outstanding economists to provide weekly analyses of the business and financial scene. At the local level the coverage is still patchy, but improvement may become evident there, too, in time.

THE SPORTS BEAT

Another area of the news in which reporter-source relationships have a good deal to do with the character of the news on the media channels is the sports beat. Here several different shaping forces are at work.

As in so many other areas, there are the ubiquitous freebies. Press box passes are a relatively legitimate, harmless form of accommodation extended to sports writers and broadcasters by both amateur and professional sports organizations. Sometimes, however, the reporter receives not only his or her press box spot, but also a fistful of choice tickets for seats down in the stands, to be handed around the newsroom or studio; that crosses the line into freebie territory and most sports editors and directors now ban acceptance of surplus tickets.

There are other fringe benefits for the sports writer willing to accept them. Many teams, both amateur and professional, offer to pay the fares of sports writers accompanying the team on the road or to spring training camp. Meals and drinks are freely available in the press box or in special clubrooms, although virtually all sports writers have expense accounts from the home office. Special assignments to write blurbs for game programs are sometimes offered sports writers, along with a comfortable honorarium for the effort.

Sports writers for large newspapers, magazines, networks, and major market broadcast outlets typically avoid all such entanglements—often because their editors or producers insist that they do so. But writers and broadcasters for smaller operations may have neither the ethical nor the economic backing of their superiors, and thus succumb more readily to the freebies. When they do, they put their integrity as unbiased reporters into question, and the consumer of news has a right to wonder whether the report in the newspaper columns or the TV broadcast is honest or slanted. The familiar saw, "Whose bread I eat, his song I sing," shadows reporters who accept a seat at the freebie table.

However, the news consumer must realize that sports news often is shaped by factors that have nothing to do with freebies or any other form of bribery of reporters. The very nature of sports reporting leads the writer or newscaster covering a particular team to identify with the fortunes of that team. If, day after day, you interview and joke with the players, mingle with the managers and coaches, and share in the exultation of victory or the drab hour of defeat, you almost inevitably become an adjunct member of the team. When the team does well, you share vicariously in that success; you get more by-lines, more space in the paper, more time on the air. When things go sour you find yourself wanting to prop up the organization, make excuses, build morale among players and fans alike. It takes a very independent sports writer to withstand this kind of involvement, to write critically and with a clear eye no matter how the breaks come for the team. The question is not one of freebies or bribery in this sort of situation; the attitude stems from a mutuality of interest, an overlapping of objectives and motives. And it certainly affects the shaping of the news.

Many readers and viewers are well aware of this tendency among sports writers and broadcasters; in fact, they expect it and would be angry and disgruntled if the situation were otherwise. News consumers—at least, sports news consumers—want some boosterism in the writers and broadcasters who cover their home teams. This may not result in an unvarnished news report, but perhaps they wouldn't want one. If there is a home-team slant in the news from the stadium press box or broadcast booth, it probably neither surprises nor affronts the news consumer.

MISPLACED BOOSTERISM

Reporters on the sports beat are not the only members of the news staff affected by the home-team approach to their jobs. Editors or news directors also may consciously desire to promote the welfare of the community; they may edit and play the news toward that promotional end. In so doing they may honestly believe that they act in the best interests of the city or town their publications or their channels serve; or they may have crasser motives rooted in economic realities. Much of the time, both their assumptions and their actions are open to serious question.

For example, many editors of Southern newspapers during the 1950s deliberately suppressed news of growing racial unrest in their communities. They defended this policy by claiming that it minimized the chance of further trouble by keeping potentially inflammatory tidings out of the news. They didn't want to be responsible, they claimed, for escalating violence.

Their policy was wrong at the time in terms of basic journalistic principle; the job of the news media is to provide the public with as honest and as complete a picture of reality as is possible. To misrepresent the extent of a major social movement, or to try to make it disappear by ignoring it, is to default on the fundamental journalistic obligation.

Moreover, the news blackout in many Southern cities was counterproductive even in terms of the rationale on which it was based. Suppressing news of growing black assertiveness did not decrease violence. In fact, the white population was so unprepared, so stunned when the equality movement grew too insistent to be kept out of the news, that reactions were more extreme than they might have been had the community news media reported fully and honestly from the beginning and made both black and white sectors aware of the basic changes taking place in society.

In other kinds of situations, editors sometimes shape news in an effort to protect the local economy. A deliberate policy of subordinating or excluding news of costly strikes or industrial slowdowns may seem to the editors who frame such a policy to be a proper and defensible gesture to protect local morale from collapse. But it is not defensible in the context of the journalistic ethic. And it may only delay community recognition of the problem and the launching of remedial efforts.

In one case several years ago, a nationally circulated magazine published a finding that the public water supplies in many of the country's major cities were contaminated and unfit for consumption. A later survey showed that more than half of the newspapers in the communities named instantly went on the defensive, pooh-poohed the magazine's findings, and swept the whole story under the rug. In more responsible newsrooms the decision was taken to launch a local investigation to substantiate or disprove the national story and provide local readers with a true picture of the situation in their communities.

The news media have a natural, healthy stake in promoting the interests of communities in which they function. As the communities grow and thrive, so do the media. But indiscriminate boosterism can be a disservice rather than a service, and some home-team spirit is shamelessly commercial at heart.

Almost every newspaper, no matter what its size, publishes each year one or more "progress" or "milestone" editions. These are typically stuffed with stories of growth in industry, agriculture, tourism, or whatever else happens to be the local economic backbone; accounts of new building, population expansion, and development of recreational facilities. These special editions are also fat with ads solicited from local merchants and industrial managers who can't afford not to add their voices to the general chorus of self-congratulation. Such special editions may in some modest degree shore up community spirit; their chief reason for being, however, is to swell the advertising revenues of the newspaper, and everyone involved in the operation knows it.

The boosterism factor is among those that shape the news and make the media tick. Its influence can be detected in events less obvious than the imposition of a news blackout, or the regular production of a "progress" edition.

Most communities, for example, have some sort of hallmark event built around a distinctive local asset or characteristic: a Lilac Festival, a Rose Parade, a Scandinavian Day. The amount of news column space or air time given to build-up stories in advance of such annual events is extravagant. No editor in his right mind would even try to make a case that such coverage is true news. Yet it squeezes off page one many items that the readers of the community ought to know about, but may never catch up with in the gush of promotional copy for the community celebration that is an attention-getter and a money-maker for the local commercial sector.

PUBLIC SERVICE

Lest you be left with a generally negative impression, it should be noted that much shaping of the news for the good of the community may legitimately serve that end.

The space in the paper and the time on the air used to promote the annual United Way or Community Chest drive for funds to finance local charities may not be news in the textbook sense, but it is justifiable as public service by the media.

When a news medium goes out of its way to give saturation coverage to an obscure or misunderstood issue (for example, land use planning) to enhance public understanding of that issue, a genuine public service is being performed.

Sometimes even suppression of the news may be warranted. When a kidnapping occurs and the victim's life may be endangered if the story is carried by the media, editors and broadcast news directors often cooperate to hold back until the danger is over. That is shaping the news, to be sure, but for a defensible end.

Most news media observe a policy of not publicizing the name of a rape victim to spare the individual further anguish or hazard. Most media also leave out of news accounts the names of juveniles charged with minor crimes, on the ground that to use the names might stigmatize the youngsters and propel them into further criminal activity, while partial anonymity (''partial'' because family and friends obviously would know in any case) might give them an opportunity to get back on a more responsible track.

AN UNRESOLVED DILEMMA

In the last several years there has been widespread soul-searching among media managers over a more momentous kind of news suppression: that involving news of terrorist attacks and assassination attempts. The arguments raised are to a point reminiscent of those used by Southern editors who blacked out news of racial trouble in their communities. The editors wanted their readers to believe that nothing was happening, so that passions wouldn't be aroused. Present-day editors and TV news directors are anguishing over how to report the activities of terrorists and assassins because they fear that coverage of such persons plays into their hands, giving them the public forum that they seek. All the media have been under fire from critics for their handling of such news.

Both *Newsweek* and *Time*, for example, were strongly criticized for their extensive coverage of attempts on President Gerald Ford's life by Sara Jane Moore and Lynette (Squeaky) Fromme in 1975. Fromme appeared on the covers of both magazines the week after her attempt. One critic, *New York Times* columnist William V. Shannon, observed that

> these persons yearn for sensational publicity. . . . The press, while reporting the essential facts, has a responsibility to deny them the gratification of instant celebrity.[24]*

But the magazines' editors felt that they had acted properly in covering this major news story. *Newsweek* editor Edward Kosner warned that even though reporters and editors admittedly did have to take into account the possible "contagion" effect of news coverage of assassination attempts,

> If the public comes to believe that the press is suppressing the news or manipulating it out of its own sense of public interest, the result will be paranoia.[25]*

Terrorism attacks, increasingly frequent in the last several years, raise the problem more often. Terrorists, often representing radical Palestinian, Arab, or other groups, have hijacked planes, kidnapped hostages, and conducted murderous forays against Israeli athletes at the Munich Olympic Games and innocent tourists in airports. In many such cases the terrorists appeared to be orchestrating their activities to obtain maximum press coverage, particularly television exposure. The question that faces those who must make news coverage decisions is whether to deny that coverage in the hope of discouraging the terrorists, or to carry out the journalistic obligation to report what is happening.

TV Guide published a thoughtful, searching analysis of the problem, citing the various bloody incidents precipitated by terrorists in recent years and the obvious efforts of the groups to exploit the worldwide publicity they were garnering. The magazine quoted several analysts, including Brian Jenkins, a Rand Corporation expert on terrorism:

> While terrorists may kill, sometimes wantonly, the primary objective of terrorism is *not* mass murder. Terrorists want a lot of people watching and a lot of people listening, not a lot of people dead.[26]

The magazine's editors then summarized the media dilemma:

> Serious questions thus are raised about the media's complicity, witting or unwitting, in the current wave of international terrorism. Would the violence decline if television ignored it or downplayed it? Does television fan the flames of political terrorism, or foster a contagion? Is self-censorship by TV news organizations a good idea, or even possible, given the competitive climate that exists among them? If television did censor itself, would terrorists merely escalate their outrages until the media simply could not ignore them? Is the public's right to know absolute? Is TV's right-to-report absolute, or does it have a responsibility for the effects of its reportage? Would modern terrorists exist at all if we did not live on a media-saturated planet? Are there positive steps TV can take to minimize its exploitation by terrorist initiatives?[27]

The answers to these questions could hardly be expected to be clear-cut and unambiguous. But among the ones the editors of *TV Guide* obtained were these:

From Dr. Frederick Hacker, a California psychiatrist who has served as negotiator in terrorist incidents:

> If the mass media did not exist, terrorists would have to invent them. In turn, the mass media hanker after terroristic acts because they fit their programming needs: namely, sudden acts of great excitement that are susceptible, presumably, of quick solution. So there's a mutual dependency.[28]

Raymond Tanter, a political scientist at the University of Michigan, pointed out that even if television did censor or downplay terrorist activities, clever activists would test the medium until they found the point where self-censorship broke down. "They'd simply conduct extravaganzas that could *not* be ignored."[29]

Television network news executives took firm stands on their responsibilities:

> ABC news head William Sheehan: "I don't think it's our job to decide what people should not know. The news media are not the reason for terrorism even though they may sometimes become part of the story."[30]
> CBS news president William Small: "It's always better to report than not to report. . . . The worst thing that could happen in this country—far worse than any act of terrorism—would be a loss of faith in the news reporting of television and newspapers."[31]

The stands of the network news executives parallel those voiced by their counterparts in newspapers and magazines. They are all consistent with the primary obligation of journalism to keep the public informed of whatever happens. But it is possible to envision a situation in which terrorists obtain access to atomic weapons and thus enormously increase the stakes involved in their antisocial activities. Will editors and network executives be able to maintain their policy of complete coverage if such a day comes? Or will the power to shape the news be taken from their hands, either by the terrorists or by government driven to the extremes of censorship in the effort to control the terrorist tactics?

THE HANDY STEREOTYPE

Let's turn now to another aspect of the journalist-source relationship that constantly shapes the news, although it may seldom be recognized either by the reporter or by the news source: stereotyping. Psychologists and communication theorists tell us that we all rely heavily upon stereotyping in day-to-day adjustment to life. That is, we try to fit new acquaintances or new ideas into prefabricated boxes in our minds. When we discover that someone newly met belongs to the country club, or to the Elks Club, or to the Friends of the Earth, we likely experience a sense of relief; it is possible now to pop the new person into a mental box of types we're already familiar with. The categorization may be simplistic and unfair; most persons are multifaceted, and to make a snap judgment on the basis of one facet may be to wrong them greatly. Yet such is our need to find a place for people, things, and ideas, and thus tidy up our sense of relationship to them, that we tend to lean heavily on stereotypes.

Think of yourself at a mixer or cocktail party, or joining a new crowd at work or in the apartment building to which you have just moved. As you encounter each new person there is a kind of feeling-out period. "Placer" questions are exchanged: "What sort of work are you in?" "Are you a native Californian?" "What's your major?" Soon the conversation becomes less wary, less anxious, partly because mutual interests have been discovered but also because each party has drawn from the other enough clues so that each can be fitted into a stereotypical mental box. We tend to be both intrigued by and uneasy with persons who for some reason don't fit neatly into one of these boxes. Life is too complicated for us to approach every other person as a unique individual; only if we can order the social landscape by the use of stereotyping can we function. This is true of most of us, and exaggeratedly so of people in the news business.

Journalists typically have little time to reach judgments about news sources with whom they must deal. Moreover, the shorthand style necessitated by the limited space or time available to tell the story does not allow close analysis of the character of news sources. (Such an approach is possible, of course, in long magazine profiles or 60-minute television documentaries; but few news sources receive that sort of coverage.) Thus it often happens that the reporter-source relationship is determined by stereotypical judgments made by the reporter on the basis of very limited acquaintance with the source. Thereafter, whatever news is obtained from that source is perceived by the reporter through a reference frame determined by the stereotypical assignment.

Once a news source has been categorized as "politician," "lawyer," or "blue collar," the reporter tends—usually unwittingly—to screen the comments from that source so that those selected for the news story are appropriate to the stereotype. (Naturally, if the reporter comes to know the news source well and on personal terms, the initial stereotype image may be considerably modified.) The stereotyping approach is generally not intentional or malicious on the journalist's part; it reflects what we all do in judging others, and it is intensified in the case of the reporter by craft conditions under which the news must be gathered and processed.

It should also be acknowledged that not all journalists indulge so freely in stereotyping. Many, particularly those with other than daily deadline schedules, can minimize the influence of stereotyping on the flow of the news. (Extreme and unusual examples might be such "new journalists" as Truman Capote and Gay Talese, who take months or years to probe a news event and the persons involved in it and can thus create a picture that reveals all the complexities and subtleties and is not dependent on one-dimensional stereotypes.)

Much daily journalism, however, shows the inevitable impact of stereotyping and thus cannot be said to reflect a wholly faithful impression of reality. Sit down with a newspaper sometime and note the incidence of tell-tale stereotypical labels fixed on individuals mentioned in the news columns: "redneck conservative," "Wall Street lawyer," "jet-setter," "Ivy League graduate," "hippie drop-out," "union boss."

Notice, too, the occasional feature story about the truck driver who loves to listen to classical music when he gets home, or about some other person who departs somehow from the stereotype assigned to him or her. The tone of such stories is frequently wondering, incredulous: "Look at this oddball I've found. . . ."

To understand how the media tick we must recognize that reliance upon stereotyping is one of the forces that shape the news—not, let it be stressed again, necessarily from any evil motivation on the part of the journalist, but simply because this is one aspect of human behavior common to all of us, including reporters, and because the deadlines of the newsgathering and -disseminating business make stereotypes so handy, even essential.

IS THAT POWER USED?

Another reporter-source relationship frequently noted in consumer complaints about news coverage and in critiques by analysts of the press is the degree to which journalists exploit their strategic position at the controls of the news media to indulge personal spites or promote pet causes. We noted earlier that one motivation drawing persons to media jobs is the power associated with those jobs. It is a truism that one does not acquire power simply for the sake of holding it unused; power affords gratification as it is wielded.

To what degree do persons in the media use their power, and for what purposes? How often do reporters, editors, or newscasters let their personal feelings show in the news decisions they make, in order to praise a friend or skewer an enemy? How often, and how much, is the news thus distorted?

There are classic instances of the use of power, both past and present. The first William Randolph Hearst attempted to use his chain of newspapers to make himself president; the contemporary William Loeb of the *Manchester Union-Leader* regularly uses his paper to whale away at political targets in the most vituperative terms. But how about less celebrated power brokers? The reporter has power, too, in the field where initial decisions are taken about what details will make news and which will be left out. The desk person in the city room and the film editor at the TV studio also have power to reshape the news as it goes through their hands. How often do they?

Unless you have worked in one of the media it is very difficult to frame answers to such questions. Almost any external observer is likely to detect what he or she perceives to be clear evidence of reportorial bias or editorial tampering. Whether there truly is bias or just a difference in judgment of news values may be known only to the persons who wrote and edited the stories in question.

Vermont Royster, former editor and columnist for the *Wall Street Journal,* points out:

> Possibly there is some conscious bias from some reporters, an intentional effort to use the news to promote their own social or political views. No doubt there is even more unconscious bias, simply because reporters partake of the passions of their times; if more of them are politically Democratic than Republican, if many are cynical about government or business or other institutions of society, they are but sharing prevalent attitudes. It would be surprising if some of this, now and then, did not unwittingly creep into their reporting. Newsmen are no less human that those who read and listen and who often see bias where none exists. . . .[32]

Efforts have been made to pin down evidence of the nature and extent of deliberate bias in the news accounts of reporters or newscasters. Newspaper coverage in campaign years has been measured by amount and content; one researcher even counted all the pro and con references to candidates in the newscasts of an entire campaign, in an effort to establish that commentators and newscasters were deliberately stacking the decks by using more negative words and phrases about conservative political candidates than about liberals, and more favorable references to liberals than to conservatives. (The study was based on the premise mentioned earlier in this book that media managers are typically conservative while "working" journalists, those in rank-and-file staff positions, are politically liberal.) Such studies done in recent years have not conclusively shown bias, although similar studies of newspaper content a couple of decades ago did reveal considerable deck-stacking.

Yet anyone who has been a reporter or editor, a TV journalist, or a magazine writer knows of many instances in which individual journalists or groups of them used the power of their positions to advance a personal cause or punish an actual or perceived enemy. Out of my own dozen years in the media, for example, I can cite some instances based on first-hand experience. I remember a reporter who, exasperated by a succession of assignments to "rubber chicken" luncheon meetings, deliberately built a story that ridiculed the speaker and exaggerated the self-conscious rituals of the civic group he was covering. It was a "that'll show 'em" reaction.

I remember, too, a city hall reporter who took himself so seriously that he demanded that a secretary be fired because she failed to usher him at once into the mayor's presence when he arrived to pose some questions. The woman *was* fired, since the reporter had so much leverage that the politician could ill afford to alienate him.

I remember a sports editor who consciously and knowingly "rode" a coach, playing up mistakes and missteps and ignoring instances of good team management, until the coach was obliged to resign.

I remember a drama reviewer for a small-city paper who regularly praised local little theater productions that featured his close friends, although he would privately admit that the shows were turkeys.

I remember the editor of a major Midwest metropolitan paper who told me that he stacked the letters-to-the-editor section of his newspaper with faked letters supporting the editorial positions advanced by the paper, in an effort to suggest a nonexistent community backing for his stands.

Most people who have worked for the media of mass communication could list a similar variety of instances in which individual journalists used the power of their positions to promote their biases.

Howard K. Smith, for many years a newsman for CBS, then ABC, criticized his colleagues on all the networks for what he saw as their tilt toward a liberal viewpoint: "If Ronald Reagan says something, it's bad, regardless of what he says. Well, I'm unwilling to condemn an idea because a particular man said it. Most of my colleagues do just that."[33]

Author and journalist T. H. White recalls that when traveling the campaign trail, gathering material for his book *The Making of the President, 1968,* he had a camera crew working independently making film for his movie version of the book. When he finally found time to edit the film for the movie, White discovered that the camera crew had been composed entirely of young people who greatly admired Robert Kennedy and Eugene McCarthy, candidates for the Democratic nomination that year, and who had no use whatever for Hubert Humphrey, who finally won the nomination. White found that on all the film recorded by his camera crew, not a foot of material showed Humphrey in a favorable pose, while every shot of either Kennedy or McCarthy was lovingly composed to show those two campaigners at their best.

Such is the evidence, more anecdotal than scientific, that journalists now and then make deliberate use of their position of power to shape the news for personal ends. But it is also true that such abuse is not well regarded by most persons in the media; it is considered outside the pale of the journalistic ethic, something to be condemned.

In late 1976, for example, the *Los Angeles Times* printed a story accusing members of the staff of the nearby *Long Beach Independent Press-Telegram* of just such an offense. Charged the *Times:*

> Top executives of Long Beach's only daily newspaper played active roles in key governmental decisions while the newspaper shielded much of the city's business from public view. . . . For more than a decade few major decisions were made at City Hall unless the newspaper approved. . . .

Newsweek quoted an unidentified member of the Long Beach newspaper's staff as admitting that the *Times* story was "essentially right" but contending that "there are people here who are clean, honest reporters who tried to get these kinds of stories in the paper. . . ."[34]

From my own experience I recall one financial editor of a major newspaper who was summarily fired from his job when it was discovered that he was printing numerous stories favorable to a company that had made an advance agreement to hire him as a consultant a year or two hence.

There is no substantial body of research data dealing with the incidence of journalists' use of their power to put down those they dislike, or promote the interests of news sources they find congenial. But a study by a Stanford University communication professor, Dan G. Drew, provided one bit of encouraging evidence.

Professor Drew set up an experimental situation in which one group being studied held negative opinions about an individual who was a news source and the other group was favorable toward the source. Drew added another variable—whether the reporters being tested were likely to encounter the source again. In other words, the study aimed to learn whether reporters who disliked the source and didn't expect to encounter him again would deal more harshly and prejudicially with the news source in their stories than would reporters who liked the source and did expect to encounter him again in their work.

Drew's conclusions from the study were that the reporters' attitudes toward the source did *not* affect their stories about that source. Nor did the expectation that the reporter would or would not later encounter the same source have an appreciable effect on the nature of the stories written.[35]

Admittedly, this is a single experiment, limited in application. But its findings agree with the less scientific observations accumulated during my professional media experience. And they accord with another observation made by Vermont Royster in the article quoted a few pages back. He said that reporters and editors today are much more conscious of their responsibility to be unbiased, and to avoid misuse of their power, than was the case in earlier eras of American journalism.

So let me offer, as a personal and subjective opinion to be discounted as you wish, the conclusion that there are indeed occasions when the news is shaped by a reporter's pique, an editor's political leaning, or a management policy (as at Long Beach), but this is emphatically *not* the norm. The typical journalist's intent is to be as fair as is humanly possible, and not to wield a media big stick for personal ends.

SUMMARY

This chapter has probed various reporter-source relationships involving beats other than government.

We have seen how, in reporting news of business and industry, journalists are often overmatched in terms of basic knowledge of the field, and also subject to tempting enticements to accept favors from news sources. Such acceptance erodes the reporter's independence and integrity.

The "home-team" psychology has been explored, both as it may affect sports writers and also as it may influence other reporters and editors to adopt an overly protective attitude toward community interests when negative news about those interests is encountered.

We have reviewed situations in which news management, even including suppression, is legitimately warranted to save a life or to shield the sensitivities of a crime victim.

We noted the agonizing decisions that confront editors and producers when a particular kind of news "source"—the criminal or terrorist—attempts to exploit media coverage to gain attention for a cause, and thus forces the media managers to consider whether they are becoming accomplices in the terrorism if they do provide such coverage.

The influence of the stereotype on the shape of the news was cited, together with the craft conditions in newsgathering and disseminating that make reliance upon stereotypes almost a necessity for journalists.

And we tried to estimate how much individual reporters and editors manipulate media power—one of the attractions of the field—to further personal causes or vendettas.

Each of these various media-source relationships influences the shaping of the news as it enters the media stream and is processed through the channels to the consuming public. In some cases, the changing and touching up of news realities may be insignificant; in other cases, built-in checkpoints in the news processing chain (the city desk, the copy editor) catch and correct what tilting has taken place; but in other cases, the alterations may be radical and they may persist all the way to the printed page or the moment of broadcast. In those latter instances, the result may be that we receive from the media a seriously distorted impression of what is going on in the world, the nation, or the community in which we live.

Let me reiterate, to be sure that no false impression has been left: the sea changes that may take place in the news as it is gathered and processed for eventual distribution to consumers are typically not the deliberate result of malicious distortion. Sometimes, yes; but usually not. Most news reaches us in a form more faithful to the reality than might well be expected, considering the many persons and complex processes involved.

Our inventory in this section of relationships between news media and news sources and their impact on the shaping of the news could be extended considerably; it would be easy to fill a book on this topic alone. But other forces also make the media tick. Let's move on to some of them in the next section.

SECTION THREE
THE MEDIA
AND
THEIR CONSUMERS

Up to this point, as we have spread the news media out on the examining table and attempted to identify the forces that make them tick, we have emphasized the significance of various relationships between the news media and other elements of society with which they interact.

We have tried to determine how and how much these interrelationships affect the shape of the news transmitted by the media. In the process we have looked into economic pressures, exemplified by advertisers and by ownership preoccupied with the bottom line. We have noted how the media relate to government and to various other news sources, and in what manner these intertwined networks of relationships determine the final form of the news as it is served up to us in the pages of the morning newspaper, in the 60 minutes of nightly network and local news, and in the pages of the newsmagazines.

In this section the emphasis will also be on relationships, but on ones that are not exactly comparable with those we have been considering so far. The relationships between media and advertisers, between media and sources, and the internal relationships among the various echelons within a single media channel are directly interactive, two-way in nature. The ad salesperson for the newspaper or the time salesperson for a broadcaster sees advertising clients daily or weekly to solicit their purchases; news reporters contact regular sources at city hall or the chamber of commerce frequently. There is ample opportunity for direct and repeated interchange;

both advertisers and sources can make their play to influence the media and shape the news.

But the relationship between media and consumers is, for the most part, a one-way arrangement. The media act upon consumers daily, even hourly. Far more rarely do consumers provide feedback in a form that affects the performance of the media or the shape of the news.

Certainly there is a media-consumer relationship. But it is largely an arm's-length affair, with all the clout on the side of the media. There are some points of occasional direct contact, and some efforts to coordinate consumer reactions so that they will make an impression on the media managers; we'll examine those as we go along. But we shall also look at the topic of media and consumers in a broader, more general context, and not so much in terms of head-to-head confrontation, as has been the case with media relationships with other elements in society.

This section will explore, in succession, the kinds of services that consumers want and need from the news media (bear in mind that "want" and "need" are not synonymous); the capability of those media to provide such services; the degree to which that capability is being used to meet consumers' wants and needs; and methods of recourse for consumers when the media fail to meet public needs, or when they actually injure the rights of individuals or groups.

7
What Media Consumers Need and Want

Charles Kuralt of the CBS program "On the Road" once observed that "journalism, by its nature, really is crisis-ridden. The country, by its nature, really is not."[1] Underlying Kuralt's perceptive comment was the recognition that the news media are not always in tune with the consumers they serve. The members of the public who buy newspapers or newsmagazines, or who turn on TV or radio newscasts, look to the media to satisfy certain felt wants. But the news content of the media is selected and presented by the media managers partly to satisfy what the media people believe are the public's *wants,* and partly to meet what journalists feel is their obligation to provide information the public *needs* to function effectively in a representative democracy. The two perceptions—that of the consumer and that of the media managers—do not necessarily coincide.

What do consumers of the news media want and expect to get from the media? Since "consumers" embraces a vast, heterogeneous group in the case of the news media, we must talk in terms of generalizations and theories. The expectations of any single consumer of media products may differ radically from those of any other; there is no way to catalog all types separately.

Most textbook writers and media analysts agree that the public consciously seeks from the media of mass communication three things: information and ideas; entertainment, in various forms; and advertising messages, as clues to products and services that may be useful. Consumers draw upon the various media differently for these three wants. Television and radio are the chief providers of entertainment; television is the principal source of nonlocal news for many; and newspapers and newsmagazines provide local and analytical news. All the media carry advertising that helps consumers choose among the many offerings in the marketplace.

The compartmentalization is not, of course, quite that neat and tight. Magazines and newspapers provide entertainment, although they are not the media chiefly relied upon for that ingredient. And the broadcast media, particularly television, to some degree provide analysis and opinion, although many consumers normally turn to the print media for such extended treatment of the news scene.

A number of social scientists have undertaken more sophisticated analyses of the functions that mass communication serves in contemporary society.

Harold Lasswell, political scientist and researcher, looking broadly at interpersonal and mass communication, concluded that three important social functions are carried out through the various levels of communication:

Providing a watch on the environment and alerting the public to threats or problems developing in the world;

Coordinating and categorizing the various elements of the social structure, so that members of the public can comprehend the forces with which they must cope to survive and prosper;

Handing on from one generation to the next the knowledge and ideas that represent our cumulative cultural heritage.

Lasswell did not contend that *mass* communication media were fully responsible for carrying out these several functions. The first two he envisioned as shared by government and the journalistic media; the third he assigned to the educational system and to some extent to the family circle.

Later analysts (Wilbur Schramm, Melvin DeFleur) suggested that the media of mass communication share increasingly in *all three* functions, and in addition provide media consumers with entertainment of various kinds.

It would be difficult to argue with that thesis. In our time the media of mass communication are pervasive, ubiquitous influences on our lives, almost from birth.

The surveillance function is performed for most of us by the headline bulletins on the morning radio news as we confront the bathroom mirror, bleary-eyed, to shave or brush our teeth. Those brief early-morning snippets reassure us that the world hasn't blown up overnight, even though a plane may have crashed in France or the stock market dipped in New York. Later, the fuller accounts in the newspaper elaborate on the bulletins, providing the detail we need to make more sense of the initial swing of the media radar. The evening TV news once more searches the news horizons, permitting us to go off to bed with a general sense of what crises are pending or waning, what problems or triumphs must be met on the morrow.

Other media perform the surveillance function, too. Long, thoughtful articles in specialized magazines give us intimations of far-reaching changes in the world, of the kind not often signaled by the dramatic upheavals that are the stock in trade of the daily media.

All of the various communication media are equally important to us in making sense of what William James called the "blooming, buzzing confusion" that surrounds us. By their headlines, by the placement and length of stories in the evening newscast, the media help to order in importance both events and personalities. They help us to categorize. Since we can't attend to *everything* that is going on, the media provide us with clues to those things of particular significance to us individually, so that we can focus on matters that affect us most nearly. This is Lasswell's second function: ordering the environment, putting it in understandable relationship.

As for the third function—transmitting the cultural heritage—the schools and the family still play significant roles. But in those roles both agencies make extensive use of the longest-established mass medium: books. And in an era when children spend two or three times as many hours being educated by the television set as by the traditional educators assigned by society, it may well be that they learn more of their heritage from that mass medium than from any other source (however flawed the lesson may be). This is particularly true since TV has access to children during the several important formative years before the schools have a chance to begin their ministrations.

The suggestion by Schramm and other leading communication scholars that the mass media do share in all three of Lasswell's functions of communication is persuasive. The analysts' further contention that the media also provide consumers with entertainment is readily accepted. However, in this text we are not much concerned about the entertainment content of the media; our focus is on the *news* media and the services they provide to the public.

How well do the scholars' perceptions of the functions of the news media coincide with what the media consumers want the media to provide?

So far as the surveillance function is concerned, there is agreement between the social scientists and the consumers. Newspaper readers and TV watchers do indeed consciously depend on the mass media for signals of hazards, changes, and opportunities in the world—both distant early warnings and instant alarms. Some tidings come through interpersonal communication at work places, at school, or at home—but in most instances those tidings originate with the media before entering the channels of interpersonal communication.

The second and third media functions on the list, ordering the environment and transmitting our cultural heritage, are also important to the consumers of the mass media, but not so consciously sought by them as are the watchtower signals.

In some cases we media consumers do turn deliberately to newspapers or broadcasters for help in putting the world into meaningful order. We read editorials or columns for insight into the meaning of events or the motivations of candidates. We turn on the newscast to find out which are the major stories of the day; we watch "Meet the Press" or "Face the Nation" to take the measure of a national figure being put on the spot. But much of the time the ordering function of the media is one that we absorb in passing, without having been aware of the need for such help and without having reached out specifically to obtain it.

Even less, perhaps, do consumers acknowledge the transmission-of-culture function of the media. Parents fret over the amount of violence to which their children are exposed by television programs; individuals vow to stop spending so many hours in front of the tube; others lambaste the newspapers for depicting a distorted version of contemporary life.

But most of us probably don't appreciate the significance of the media as educative forces. We probably don't comprehend how instantaneously the media can infuse new cultural concepts into society, like fast-spreading dye in a tub of water. Changes in fashion, manners, morals, and life styles may not be created by the media, but their rapid dissemination *is* a consequence of mass media functioning. And many fads gradually evolve into integral elements of our cultural heritage.

Perhaps it is fair to say that most media consumers have a vague, uneasy sense that the media are powerful educative forces, shapers of cultural change. But if questioned, most would still cite schools, family, and churches as the chief guardians and transmitters of the cultural heritage. In this perception they are not at odds, really, with the social scientists, who contend, after all, only that the mass media *share* in the function of education and the transmission of cultural values, not that the media have taken over full responsibility.

In the course of our overall examination of how the media tick, it has been necessary to take some time to consider the functions of the media as they have been identified by the leading analysts in this field and also as they are generally perceived by the consumers who are served by the media products. How efficiently do the media perform their various functions in society? How diligently is the watchtower manned? How reliable is the media radar upon which we all rely? How well do the media dispel the "blooming, buzzing confusion" for readers and viewers, helping them to make sense of it all? What effects—good and bad—do the media have as educative agents, transmitters and even molders of cultural standards and values? In chapter 8 we'll try to find at least some of the answers to these and like questions.

8
How Well Are Media Consumers Served?

Chapter 7 identified some of the services that consumers expect of the news media, and discussed the social scientists' formulations of the functions performed by communication in general and the mass media in particular for society as a whole.

This chapter considers how effectively the media serve consumers and perform social functions. We'll focus chiefly on three aspects of the media: their role as sentinel, bringing tidings of the outside environment; their role as coordinator of the confusing glut of events about us; and their role as transmitter of cultural and other values.

As we noted in chapter 7, media are also important to consumers as providers of entertainment and advertising messages. But our chief concern in this book is with the news content of media; entertainment contributions of the media and the special functions of advertising will be considered in other books in this series.

MANNING THE WATCHTOWER

Consumers and scholars agree on the importance of the surveillance function of the news media. Social scientists see it as an essential function of journalistic communication; consumers consciously reach out for this service from one or more of the news media.

Several considerations determine how effectively the various news media perform the watchtower or surveillance function. Most obvious and perhaps most important is the limited size of the news package that the media are technologically able to deliver to their readers, listeners, or viewers. The "news hole" of a newspaper is that space left after advertising, comics, and special interest features such as crossword puzzles and bridge columns are accounted for. Into this space reporters and editors fit watchtower news from all quarters of the compass, including news of sports, business, and community activities such as announcements of meetings, weddings, births, and deaths.

The news hole obviously varies in size with the overall paper. A major metropolitan daily has a news hole of many columns; the editor of a small community paper may have at his disposal only a few. But the metro attempts to survey a far broader horizon than does the community paper, so the difference in column inches available may not be particularly significant. The important point is that the news hole on any paper is woefully inadequate in terms of the surveillance function the paper is expected to perform. Remember James Reston's comment, quoted in an earlier chapter, that even the hefty *New York Times,* with the largest news hole of any American daily, has space to publish each day only about one-twentieth of the number of words of news that flow into its offices.

The news package is even more limited in the case of television. Most of the programming day is given over to entertainment and advertising; the showcase network newscasts occupy a half hour twice a day and local newscasts might account for an equal amount of air time. Even these relatively brief segments are interrupted by commercials, and the electronic news hole is often reduced disproportionately by extended weather reports. (A weather report is certainly a fulfillment of the surveillance function, in the classic sense; but if it takes four minutes of a net twenty-two minutes available to tell everything else, something has to give.)

Newspaper people like to point out that in the net time available on a half-hour newscast (after commercials, introductions, and sign-offs have been subtracted), the newscasters can read only about as many words as are contained in a column and a half of a newspaper page. That should not, however, be taken to mean that a half-hour newscast conveys only as much news as would a column and a half of newspaper type. Television is sight and sound as well as words, and oftentimes more is conveyed by the pictures and sound track than by all the words on the anchorperson's script.

Still, it remains true that on television as in the newspaper, packaging limits severely handicap the media's performance of the watchtower function. The consequences for the consuming public can be serious and far-reaching, as if a frontier warning post were equipped with radar that functioned only intermittently and irregularly. Sometimes the warning blips would be loud and clear; other segments of the horizon would yield only silence or static. Some of the time helpful intelligence would be gleaned to send back to the headquarters station; at other times a whole fleet of attacking missiles or bombers could approach undetected.

In more directly applicable terms, the consumers of the news media may not get word of important developments at home or abroad. This has happened often, and in our time. The American public has been taken unawares by upheavals abroad that had been signaled in advance by undercurrents of change in social and political structures—changes that were not included in the news budget because to report them would have required lengthy, detailed accounts.

The gasoline shortage of the winter of 1973–74 came as an unpleasant surprise to most Americans, although the conditions that brought it about had been evident for some years. The media had failed to cover the story.

Three researchers at the University of West Virginia studied the performance of the media during the years that preceded the crisis and found that they behaved "more like a thermometer than a barometer," reporting after the fact but failing to read the warning signals.[2] This negative judgment requires one qualification, however. Had an individual consumer been attending to *all* forms of media during the 1971–73 period, including specialized industry magazines, he or she would have been fairly adequately alerted to what was brewing. In other words, if all the media are taken into consideration, the early-warning function had been performed.

As a practical matter, however, few consumers pay attention to any but the mass media reports available through the general daily or weekly channels; specialized technical publications reach very small audiences. It is upon the mass media that we depend, and those media are frequently unable to do the watchtower job for us simply because there isn't space or time to handle certain complex issues. A student riot, good for three-quarters of a column of type in the paper or 60 seconds of TV film, is far easier to cover and to fit into the space and time segments available.

One further point should be made with respect to the watchtower function, in fairness to the media. Even when space or time may be available for satisfactorily scanning the horizons and reporting on pending developments, reporters and editors may be deterred from making the effort by the disappointing public response to earlier such attempts. Readership studies show how woefully low were the ratings for long "think" pieces, or background series on major issues developing or already confronting the country. Magazines occasionally devote entire issues to searching examination of a complex issue, and major newspapers such as the *Los Angeles Times* invest many columns of space in an extended series of thorough articles, only to discover from subsequent readership studies that hardly anyone bothered to read the magazine piece or the newspaper series. On television, documentaries have often drawn such low viewer ratings that network executives were fearful of repeating the experiment lest programs adjacent to the documentary slot also suffer.

For a variety of reasons, the surveillance function may not be carried out by the news media as completely and as expertly as would be ideal. Space and time limitations pose practical barriers. Reporters' and editors' previous experience with reader and viewer reactions dampens the incentive to undertake a serious effort to meet the sentinel obligation.

WANTING AND GETTING

The last point above leads logically to consideration of a craft condition that is built into all of the media and that affects journalists' performance overall but particularly in the sentinel role. This is the divergence between what newspeople believe consumers *want* from the media, and what newspeople believe consumers should *get* from the media.

Earlier we noted that conscientious editors try to balance the scales, putting into one pan enough of the kinds of news they believe readers want and into the other a sufficient helping of the news readers need to function as citizens. There must be enough of the "wanted" news so that readers will buy the paper and keep it afloat economically; there must be adequate servicing of the needs of readers (whether or not the readers recognize those needs) so that the journalistic obligation to inform the people is fulfilled.

How accurately do media decision makers judge what readers or viewers want? And how competent are they to determine what news readers truly need?

In determining what consumers want from the news media, editors and producers are guided by some feedback data; here is one aspect of the media-consumer relationship that is at least partially two-way. Audience ratings appear to tell television producers that viewers want lively, entertaining TV newscasts, brief reports, lots of action, not much detail—or so the "news doctors," the professional consultants, advise. That formula has been more and more widely adopted. One station staff member, responding to a query in the periodic Alfred I. DuPont–Columbia University Survey of Broadcast Journalism, wrote: "I think there is a danger of big-market journalism becoming nothing more than a rating game, reaching the lowest common denominator because of the influence of news consultants."[3]

The "happy talk" formula peddled by the consultants on the basis of their readings of the Nielsen ratings may be on the verge of moving from the individual station to the network level. When in 1976 the ABC network hired Barbara Walters as the first woman to co-anchor a major network newscast, observers both within and without the industry saw the move not as a deserved recognition of a gifted interviewer and newscaster, but as a first step toward tailoring the network news to suit supposed reader wants rather than reader needs. Walters was perceived by some, including veteran anchormen, as a show business personality rather than as a newsperson. Also, as *Newsweek* observed at the time: "Some of ABC's other plans for the show sound suspiciously like the 'happy talk' that has invaded local TV news."[4]

Trends in television news, like so many other decisions in the industry, are founded upon audience ratings that are fallible and uncertain at best. Moreover, even if ratings could be taken as exact scientific measurements of what people are watching, does it follow that they tell us what people *want* to watch? Or do the ratings reflect only which offerings *among those available* are watched by the most viewers?

The decision makers of the television news industry also ought to ask themselves whether viewer wants should be the sole arbiter of news content. If the news consultants are right and the sex–crime–happy banter mixture is what viewers want, it is nonetheless evident that newscasts built on that pattern will not provide viewers with the solid, unspectacular kinds of news they *need* if the surveillance function of the media is to be carried out.

Newspaper editors have struggled with this wants-needs balancing act a good deal longer than have television news executives. Editors have a kind of equivalent of the Nielsen ratings, in the form of readership surveys. Such surveys typically show that comics and sports are among the individual sections of the newspaper with the greatest readership. They also show that among the general news offerings, human interest feature stories and accounts of crime and sex-related incidents are most widely read.

A few editors and publishers have taken such findings as a blueprint, just as some TV news directors have taken the Nielsens as their Bible. Such editors compose their publications almost entirely of sex, crime, pictures, feature stories, and sports—and some prosper, for a time.

But most editors have sought a balance, recognizing that readership surveys have weaknesses and that the journalistic function of providing a true picture of the news must be carried out, no matter what the surveys show. The editors don't always strike that balance with precision. They have a better batting average, perhaps, than local TV news; but this reflects the priority that news has always held in the print medium mixture. The broadcast media were first and primarily entertainment media, and this emphasis persists.

In all the media, however, the continuing effort to blend the news readers want and the news readers need in a mixture both sufficiently attractive to be a commercial success and sufficiently substantial that the public's need to know will be properly served, is one of the factors that most strongly influence the shape of the final media products.

The shaping that has been taking place in recent years is not reassuring, as reflected not only in the "happy talk" TV news format but also in changing patterns in the print media.

Many newspapers across the nation have remodeled their news pages around a kind of feature magazine approach. The chief ingredients are long personality feature stories; many large, space-consuming picture displays; and a consequent shrinkage in the attention given to "hard" news the public needs to know and to the homely bulletin-board items that only the newspapers have the means to supply.

We noted in chapter 3 the upsurge of emphasis on gossip of all kinds in both magazines and newspapers, including some of the nation's most respected journals. Evidence crops up, too, that newspaper executives are deliberately infusing more crime and sex into the news columns as they feel the need to match TV formula news packaging. A Detroit editor recently sent to his staff a memo that directed, in part:

> I want at least one, preferably two or three stories on [page] 1A that will jolt, shock, or at least wake up our readers. Go through the last few weeks of the early edition and you'll see what I want: "Nun charged with killing her baby," "Prison horrors revealed," "They chummed together—and died together." Sure, we've got to cover the hard news—but you've got the whole rest of the paper for all but the hardest news. Look for sex, comedy, and tragedy. These are the things readers will talk about the next day—and that's what I want. . . .[5]

It seems reasonable to ask: Are the news media faithfully serving the sentinel function when the scales tip more and more in the direction of mixing the news to match consumer wants rather than consumer needs? Is it time for media owners and decision makers to take a searching look at the rationale for their decisions about what readers and viewers want and what readers and viewers need? Such decisions are among the most important ones being made today in any sector of society. Those who make them have a greater responsibility than any of them appear willing to acknowledge.

ALL THE WORLD A POLICE BEAT?

One other craft condition has much to do with the effectiveness with which news media perform the sentinel or surveillance function. It is the tendency of many journalists in all the media to be governed by the "police beat syndrome"—covering all forms of news as though they were similar in nature to the kinds of incidents that crop up on the police blotter. Those incidents are typically violent and episodic. They represent social aberrations, sharp departures from the norm, typically resulting in some form of injury to the community. Also, each can usually be wrapped up in a single account, given its allotted space in the paper or time on the air, and then forgotten until the trial comes along—a neat, quick, simple assignment for the reporter.

Considering the nature of the events being treated, police beat coverage is efficient and probably satisfactory from the standpoint of the consumer and of society as a whole—so long as it is confined to police news. But when the same approach is applied to other forms of news, the fit may be poor.

Many types of news cannot be reported as one-shot eruptions of violence. As James Reston of the *New York Times* once put it, this is "an age of ambiguity, and we [the press] are not very good at handling ambiguity."

We noted in chapter 5 how reliance by journalists on official sources often causes them to overlook news developments that have no official spokespersons or highly visible leaders. Reliance on the police beat syndrome as a method of reportage similarly causes journalists to miss important news that is difficult to understand and complicated to write about. If the story can be pegged on a riot, a terrorist attack, or a palace coup (a police beat aspect), it may be covered. If it's a slow-burning fuse, or a drawn-out discussion of a subject inherently unexciting (by police beat standards), it may receive a lick and a promise or no mention at all. Other topics that fit conveniently into the police beat format get the space instead.

The Reverend David K. McMillan, an Ohio Presbyterian minister, told his parishioners that during the last 20 years they and he had

> lived in a world of never-ending crises. A few have been genuine, but many have finally revealed themselves as little more than sensationalized incidents reported in exaggerated terms by public media which appear to have lost their sense of proportion in clamoring for our attention. . . . I remember my own frustration in searching vainly, day after day, for the slightest mention in the local paper of the special session of the United Nations General Assembly dealing with world hunger—and I remember also my frustration in wading through columns without number reporting the media-created sensation which was something called the Symbionese Liberation Army.[6]

Charles Kuralt of the CBS network complained about journalists' "fascination with the entertainer, the politician, and the criminal." He continued, in a commencement address delivered in New York:

> I wonder, in spite of the evidence of our headlines to the contrary, whether humaneness, and decency, and the will for justice, are not, in fact, becoming stronger than ever in our national life, and if that will not be seen, someday, to have been the really significant development in the time of the Selma marches, the Tet offensive, and the Nixon tapes.[7]

The police beat approach to covering news is attractive to the journalist since it represents a quick, undemanding way to whip a story into shape before deadline or air time. If a particular news situation can't be shoehorned into the package format, it is forgotten. At that point the watchtower radar breaks down, and we media consumers fail to learn tidings that could be significant to both our present and our future, if any. At the least, we get an incomplete and distorted picture of reality.

ORDERING THE CONFUSION

Although it is not always performed as effectively as we might wish, the sentinel function of the news media is indispensable to us. The same could be said of the second social function scholars assign to the media: helping us make order of the people and events that swirl in and out of our ken day by day.

Only a hermit could undertake the ordering job unaided. The rest of us live in the midst of the confusion; we must contend with a world far more complex than the hermit's simple surroundings. We need a program or a scorecard to identify the players and their positions in the global or national competitions for power, notice, wealth, or office. Without the assistance of the news media, we would be befuddled social drop-outs.

Frank K. Kelly, an experienced analyst of the press, eloquently describes the journalist engaged in carrying out the ordering function:

> Often it seems that our society is a tremendous cave of sound, in which voices bounce back and forth, calling to one another, responding to one another, stimulating one another. The journalist stands in the middle of this huge, roaring chamber, trying to catch the most significant voices, the rising new voices, the receding old voices. As he listens, he must think—think for himself, forming his own judgments out of all the pieces of his knowledge of the past and the present; and think for the public, for the millions who rush from the confusion of their private lives to the perplexities of trying to be citizens of the world.[8]

The historian identifies for us the significant persons and events of the past. The journalist must do the same in the present and on the fly, helping the media consumer to recognize the figures of interest or importance (not necessarily the same thing), the issues of significance, the fads, the fakes, the crises, and the crusades—and then helping to put all of them in some sort of meaningful relationship to each other.

It is a massive job of identification and categorization we expect of the news media. By and large, we as consumers are fairly well served by the media's ordering of the confusion, *provided* we take the trouble to attend to the various media messages. It is unrealistic to depend upon one medium alone— say, television, which is the chief source of news and ideas for many of us. If consumers truly want to benefit from the scorecard help of the news media in making sense of the world, they must draw upon the resources of *all* the media, or at least more than one or two.

Consumers also must recognize the forces and factors that limit or modify the effectiveness with which journalists carry out the ordering function. One such factor—journalists' dependence on the stereotype—was discussed at some length in an earlier chapter. It isn't only journalists who make use of stereotypes, of course; we all depend on them as handy devices for fitting people and things into place on a spectrum. But the deadlines that oblige journalists to make identifications and reach judgments in that "huge, roaring chamber" in a matter of minutes or hours force them to rely heavily on stereotypical shorthand. That reliance may lead to oversimplified decisions and inadequate identifications.

News media reliance on stereotypes is illustrated in the extreme in the work of political cartoonists. Political cartoons have no room for subtleties and shadings; the images are strong, memorable—and sometimes savagely distorted. In the reporter's extended story, or the newscaster's comments, the distortion may be nowhere near so great as in the cartoonist's work. But to the degree any journalist does depend, as all must, on stereotypes to do some of the job of categorizing, there will inevitably be some warping of reality. As we turn to the media for scorecard help, this is one limiting factor we need to bear in mind.

OBJECTIVITY—
A MISUNDERSTOOD CONCEPT

Another limitation is the degree of detachment and objectivity journalists bring to their jobs. I hesitate to bring up the term "objectivity," since it has been a whipping boy for so long in discussions of the functioning of the press. The word has been misused and abused so frequently that it evokes knee-jerk reactions whenever it is introduced in conversations with media persons. Yet we should make an effort to clarify the significance of the concept, partly because it *is* so ubiquitous in shop talk among journalists and partly because the rationale behind it is still meaningful in media performance.

In some earlier eras of American journalism we find little mention of objectivity. Newspapers of Colonial days and during much of the nineteenth century made no pretense of being objective. That characteristic was not expected of them. They were organs of a political party, or megaphones to amplify an owner's causes; news was blended freely with opinion, and distortion and suppression were commonplace. Under the libertarian philosophy that shaped the First Amendment there was nothing untoward in all this. Newspapers were to be free, not necessarily responsible, balanced, or objective.

Only when the numbers of newspapers dwindled and ownership became concentrated in the hands of relatively few individuals did the libertarian notions come to be modified by the concept of social responsibility. The social responsibility theorists argued that since the channels of communication were few, they must be impartial and unbiased. The free and open marketplace of ideas no longer prevailed (if it ever had), and thus the few persons who were privileged to have access to the news media should be expected to offer unadulterated goods to the public. News should be objectively reported; opinion should be labeled and segregated.

The newspapers (then the only mass medium, other than magazines) gradually accepted the social responsibility obligation, some more earnestly and consistently than others. Through much of the current century, reporters and editors—and, in their time, newscasters—gave allegiance to the ideal of objective reporting. But it was often an uneasy, even hypocritical allegiance, for anyone who gave the matter serious thought had to conclude that the ideal was in practice unattainable. What point was there in pledging fealty to a concept that could not be realized?

The questioners were right in their basic assumption: objectivity *is* out of reach. None of us can ever be truly objective; too many biases, beliefs, and experiences are built into our backgrounds for us to be completely objective about anything or anybody. But does it necessarily follow that we ought to junk the concept altogether?

Being "objective" is very much like being "truthful." Quote marks belong about both terms, for the same reasons. Most of us like to think of ourselves as truthful persons; truth is a tenet of right conduct in most philosophies. Yet as a practical matter none of us is completely truthful; if we were, we'd swiftly become insufferable. All of us get through life by using untruths of varying kinds as lubricants in our relationships with other persons. We tell social lies frequently: "We'd just love to come, but we're already tied up that evening." "Helen, you haven't aged a bit!" "What a beautiful baby!" We tell compassionate lies, too: "Nonsense, Uncle Fred, you'll be out of that bed and back on your feet in no time." "It's really striking; you have great promise as an artist." And we tell defensive lies: "The check is in the mail." "Actually, Officer, I was doing well under 30." If we think of them as untruths at all, we excuse them as necessary "white lies" and still argue that we are basically truthful persons who would not traffic in serious falsehood.

One of my colleagues recalls that his mother told him: "Son, if you find you have to lie, stay as close to the truth as possible." That is very much the situation of journalists who adhere to the concept of objectivity. As a practical matter, they are aware that they can't be wholly objective; but they *can* try to come as close to the ideal as possible.

Just as most of us know we can't be completely truthful, but hope to be close most of the time, so many reporters contend that it is better to aim at the objective ideal, even if you will inevitably fall short of the mark, than it is to abandon the effort and allow bias free rein.

In an address at the University of Texas, Walter Cronkite spoke for many of his colleagues in both print and broadcast media:

> I do not want to leave you with the impression that I think we are perfect. Far from it. We make many errors. We do things we ought not to do, and we leave undone things we ought to do. We are not *always* fair and just. There is not a man who can truthfully say that he does not harbor in his breast prejudice, bias,

strong sentiments pro and con on some if not all the issues of the day. Yet it is the distinguishing character of the professional journalist that he can set aside these personal opinions in reporting the day's news. None of us succeeds in this task in all instances, but we know the assignment and the pitfalls and we succeed far, far more often than we fail—or than our critics would acknowledge.[9]

It is important to realize that those journalists who cling to the notion that it is best to try to hew as closely as possible to the ideal of objectivity are more dependable guides to understanding society than are those who have decided to become advocates (on the model developed by Morris Janowitz, which we discussed in chapter 4). Advocacy journalists, who scorn the concept of objectivity as outworn and hypocritical, approach the task of ordering the confusion as an opportunity to identify ''good guys'' and ''bad guys'' according to a special-interest scorecard. The categorizations they make tend to reflect the causes in which they have enlisted, rather than the ideal of objectivity. Their credentials for carrying out the ordering function of the media are to that extent flawed.

Some persistent critics of the press—and even a few media practitioners—have cited other reasons why the media may not be performing the functioning of ordering the confusion as well as they might.

ARE JOURNALISTS IN TOUCH WITH THE PUBLIC?

In 1969 the then vice president, Spiro Agnew, unleashed the first of his direct attacks on the media. In a speech that sent tremors through all of the press he asserted that ''a small group of men, numbering perhaps no more than a dozen anchormen, commentators, and executive producers . . . decide what 40 to 50 million Americans will learn of the day's events in the nation and the world.''[10] These elite and powerful dozen, Agnew charged, were of the ''Eastern, liberal establishment.'' They lived and functioned in the artificial atmosphere of New York and Washington and were out of touch with the ideas and the needs of the American public.

In the aftermath of that Agnew speech and another very much like it that he delivered a week later, ABC network anchorman Howard K. Smith told Edith Efron of *TV Guide* in an interview that Agnew was at least partly right: ''Newsmen are *proud* of the fact that the middle class is antagonistic to them. They're proud of being out of contact with the middle class.''[11] Smith went on to quote a syndicated columnist as having said, in effect, ''Let's face it, we reporters have very little to do with middle America. They're not our kind of people.''[12]

At the annual meeting of the American Society of Newspaper Editors in

1975, educator-author Michael Novak told the assembled leaders of American newspaper journalism that they had lost touch with their real constituency, "the 90 per cent of Americans who make less than $17,000 a year, do not read *Time* or *Newsweek,* and who are not college-educated."[13] Novak described today's journalists as a well educated, highly paid elite with a built-in bias that has no relevance to the working class.

This theme has been hit often by critics of the performance of the news media. Has it any substance? The question calls for several different answers, since the criticism from which it arises has several components.

For one thing, implicit in Agnew's initial charges, echoed by others, is the notion that some sort of conspiracy exists among the news media. That aspect of the criticism can be dealt with quickly. It is simply not supported by any meaningful evidence, whether the conspiracy notion is being applied to media ownership or to the "working journalists," the women and men who gather and process the news and who are largely responsible for carrying out the function of ordering the confusion.

It is true enough that news media ownership in most cases tends to be conservative in political ideology and supportive of the status quo, as we noted in chapters 3 and 4. But this is not the consequence of conspiracy; it is rather that most media enterprises are big business. Their owners think much as do the owners of other types of big business. They do not, however, connive in a monolithic master plan such as Agnew envisioned.

If the former vice president's charges are without foundation with respect to media ownership, they apply even less to rank-and-file journalists. Media staff members are a diverse company, with neither motive nor occasion for conspiring against the citizenry. They typically share an adversary attitude toward government, particularly at the national level; but they perceive that attitude as part of their responsibility to serve the public as watchdog. Some overdo the role, admittedly, but out of individual zeal or competitiveness rather than in compliance with a secret pact.

The conspiracy aspect of the criticism leveled by Agnew and others can be set aside as inapplicable. How about the charge that the news is managed by an "effete, elite, Eastern establishment," to use Agnew's language? This attack also fails to hold up under examination.

Surveys of the ranks of journalists, including network commentators based in Washington and New York, reveal that they come from all parts of the country, small towns as well as big, backwater colleges as well as the Ivy League, and more often from the geographic section labeled middle America than from the East Coast. The same kind of diversity of background is apparent among media owners and managers.

It is also unlikely that most journalists are "proud of being out of contact with the middle class," as Howard K. Smith put it. In fact, most journalists would insist that they are very much in contact with ideological middle America.

With this much said, however, it is necessary to add a few qualifications.

The men and women who staff the news media *are* different from the majority of the consumers they serve in some significant respects. Most journalists are better educated (with at least one college degree) than are most of the persons who read the newspapers and listen to the newscasts.

Journalists other than owners and executives tend to be strongly liberal in political persuasion—unlike media consumers, who reflect a roughly half-and-half ideological breakdown.

It is worth recalling our earlier exploration of what attracts individuals to work in the news media. Among the attractions were a desire for power; a wish to be in the middle of events, to know more about what's happening in the world than almost anyone else does; and a conviction that a public service is performed by those who are gatekeepers of the news, deciding what the public will know or not know. All this suggests that journalists may at least unconsciously consider themselves different from the average citizen in that they are better informed than media consumers and engaged in a higher mission than are most other citizens.

Whether it follows from all the foregoing that journalists are doing a slanted job of ordering the confusion and categorizing the world for the benefit of media users is arguable. For what it may be worth, my opinion is that this is not a distorting factor very often or very significantly. Another criticism of journalists' effectiveness at ordering the world's events may, however, have more substance.

HOW MUCH DO JOURNALISTS KNOW?

Some critics complain that journalists do an inadequate job of sorting out the meaning and significance of events because the journalists often do not know enough about the subjects of their articles or news broadcasts.

This seems paradoxical after we have just noted that journalists are on the whole better educated than the consumers they serve. But in fact the two themes are not necessarily contradictory. A college degree may indeed make the journalist better educated than most of those who read or watch the news reports. But a college degree does not make its holder an expert in all things, and the typical journalist has to cover a variety of subjects on a given beat or in a given time span.

Vermont Royster, former editor and columnist for the *Wall Street Journal,* points out:

> No man can be well-informed on every subject, and the nature of his craft makes the newsman a professional amateur. But the problem is compounded by an all-too-prevalent habit of mind among newsmen. That habit is not to recognize what they do not know and to be content with a smattering of ignorance. They

> grow so accustomed to leaping from story to story with perhaps a quick briefing
> from the files, if that, that they are reluctant to take the time to really find out
> what they are writing about.[14]

This quick "leaping from story to story" may not cause problems for the general assignment reporter in the newsroom who covers fires, accidents, and city council meetings. But where the incidents or ideas being covered are more complicated, the reporter's superficial knowledge of the subject may be a real hindrance to accurate and informed coverage.

Sylvia Porter, the syndicated financial columnist, has decried the "economic illiteracy" of many of the reporters assigned to cover the news of business, labor, and the money market. Many city hall reporters, if pressed, will acknowledge that they really don't comprehend the intricacies of municipal finance, mil levies, or tax impact; yet they write knowingly on such subjects, and the readers or viewers assume that they are getting reliable impressions.

Even where specialists are concerned, lack of thorough knowledge may be a problem. Press analyst Edwin Diamond quotes political scientist Walter Burnham as suggesting that the 1976 campaign may have introduced an era of "politics without parties," in which, Diamond observes, "the role of mediating among factions and building up one or another of the candidates has been shifting elsewhere, principally to the press."[15] Diamond sees in this possibility a danger for the news consumer:

> I happen to think the press today is not prepared for political power. As the
> political writer Richard Reeves has pointed out, the press is essentially an
> immature institution, something like "a lovable little child. . . . It has trouble
> concentrating on more than one thing at a time."[16]

Some substantiation for Diamond's concern can be found in the typical media coverage of primary elections—coverage provided, incidentally, by some of the most expert political reporters in the business. Primaries in 1972 and 1976 were covered as though they were horse races. The underlying issues were lost sight of by those in the press bus and thus never conveyed to their readers and viewers.

Unfortunately, there is no simple or immediate solution to the problem presented by lack of extensive knowledge on the part of journalists. Some real gain is being registered by midcareer education programs such as Harvard's Nieman Fellowships and the National Endowment for the Humanities fellowships for journalists at Stanford and the University of Michigan. Each year these three programs combined bring approximately three dozen working journalists back to a campus to spend a year filling in knowledge gaps or acquiring a specialized education in a particular field they are covering. But that accounts for the upgrading of three dozen a year, of the 70,000 men and women working in newsgathering and -disseminating roles in the mass media.

The costs involved, should the various media attempt to staff all complex news beats with true experts, would be staggering. Still, some of the largest media elements have made at least some effort in that direction. The *Des Moines Register and Tribune* had as its Washington bureau chief, covering government and Supreme Court beats, an accomplished reporter who also held a law degree (Clark Mollenhoff). Television newsman Carl Stern, also based in Washington, was a lawyer. Many newspapers and newsmagazines now prefer to hire persons with both a bachelor's and a master's degree, combining journalism education with advanced specialization in some other field.

We as consumers can hope for more such enlightenment on the part of media management, and for more professional sabbatical programs such as those of the Nieman and NEH ventures. But we probably should expect that our hopes will be realized only in part, and slowly. In the meantime, the news media's function of ordering the confusion will continue to be performed unevenly, however good the intentions of the journalists who staff those media.

TRANSMITTING CULTURAL VALUES

The third function performed for consumers by the news media, according to social scientists, is the transmission of our cultural heritage from one generation to the next, and horizontally within a single generation. We shall not undertake an extended discussion of this function—not because the value-transmission function is unimportant, but because another book in the Perspectives in Mass Communication series deals with the role of the media as expressions of popular culture. That book will deal with the transmission function as well as various other aspects of media impact on social values and standards. We'll be content here to advance several general propositions, and to leave extended exploration of the topic to another book and another author.

One fundamental point about the role of the news media in transmitting values and standards: through much of their history the media have been to a significant degree supporters of the status quo. This assertion should not be interpreted narrowly. It is not based on the fact, noted earlier, that most media owners and proprietors are conservative in political outlook, or on the fact that most newspapers give editorial support to conservative rather than liberal candidates. It has a much broader application.

In a literal sense, the media of mass communication are built into the structure of things as they are. The media interact with and are interdependent with the other segments of our social and political structures. It is understandable, then, that the news media would tend to support and protect the overall structures of which they are a part.

Thus you will find media calling, say, for a change in parties in Washington or the statehouse, or for alterations in existing government policies. But you will not find any medium of mass circulation calling for a total change in the overall *system*—from a representative democracy to a fascist state, for example, or to a communist dictatorship. The news media of this country could not function under a system that curtailed freedom of expression, as would be the case in any totalitarian structure. Thus there is a clearly defined limit to the degree of change they will advocate.

The media are similarly unwilling to see sweeping changes in other fundamental aspects of our system. Consider the basic building block of our social system: the family unit. Continuation of the system of organization of the public into family units is essential to the continued survival of the media of mass communication. The advertising revenue upon which all of the media significantly depend is generated by consumption patterns tightly linked to family formation and maintenance. Thus most of the media tend to support the perpetuation of our present social system. There are, for example, few media advocates of communal child raising as it is practiced in China. And media treatment of lesser threats to the existing social organization and consumption pattern (such as minimal-outlay communes, living off the land) is likely to depict such ventures as aberrations or short-lived curiosities.

It is not at all surprising that in respect to fundamental characteristics of our system, the media support continuation of things as they are. The bacterium in a droplet of moisture, if it had a choice, would not want the droplet to dry up and bring its small world to an end. The news media are tightly woven into the present social, economic, and political structure, and it is only natural that they would resist moves to unravel that system drastically and irrevocably.

Yet is it paradoxically true—and this is the second general observation to be made about the value-transmission function of the news media—that the same media that support the outer limits of the status quo simultaneously function actively as agents of smaller degrees of change *within* those outer boundaries.

It is through the media of mass communication that fads swiftly spread; it is through the entertainment and news media that changes in moral attitudes are brought to wide attention and thus given a chance to "take" with substantial segments of the population.

The media do not usually create new modes or attitudes on their own; they function instead as universal showcases that gradually accustom the viewing or reading public to new ideas, trends, or practices, and thus in time make those ideas, trends, or practices acceptable so that in some instances they become knit into the fabric of our cultural values.

Consider what in the eyes of some persons is increasing freedom of expression in the use in the media of once-banned words, and what in the eyes of others is a disturbing breakdown of moral standards. Words dealing explicitly with sex or obscenity used to be taboo in virtually all printed media except those furtive, under-the-counter publications considered outside the pale. Then, first in book fiction, then in magazine fiction, then in nonfiction articles or interviews in magazines, the forbidden words infiltrated the print media. At each stage public shock appeared to be less and objections fewer.

Newspapers of general circulation remained the last unbreached bastion (except for a few isolated quotes from literature or from official reports on urban violence) until the Nixon tapes surfaced during the final stages of Watergate. The tapes were considered so important to the public's right to know for other reasons that many editors (though not all) ran transcripts containing words rarely before seen in the nation's general press. Some papers stuck with the deletion device (_____, or . . .), and only a few television newscasters went so far as to read the objectionable passages on the air.

The still-fluid position of the general media on the question was apparent a couple of years after the Nixon tapes, when during the 1976 election campaign the then secretary of agriculture, Earl Butz, was quoted in a specialized magazine as having told a vulgar and derogatory ''joke'' about blacks. Butz was forced from office for having told the story in a private conversation with a group that included a reporter. But most of the American public never did find out exactly what it was that the cabinet officer said that cost him his job. The magazine *Rolling Stone,* another limited audience publication, many college newspapers, *New Times,* and a couple of general circulation newspapers did print the original comment. But nearly all other newspapers and all broadcast news reporters used euphemisms or the deletion device. One such newspaper observed editorially:

> Time and place mean everything. Many who sometimes use the words in question would not do so at home, in front of the kiddies or a prim mother-in-law or mother superior. . . . Nothing is gained by being gratuitously offensive or shocking.[17]

Nonetheless, it remains a fact that the news media have been substantially responsible for the spread not only of the acceptability of four-letter words but of many other once unheard-of developments (such as nudity on the stage, screen, and even television).

So, too, have the media ushered into acceptance various other, less controversial changes in manners, modes, and fashions. In this context they are indeed instruments of change in society's values.

THE PENDULUM SWINGERS

From time to time in earlier chapters we have mentioned the ''new journalists.'' New journalism embraces a number of forms of experimentation intended by the experimenters to supplement, replace, or improve upon the kind of journalism rigidly based on the concept of objectivity.

Among the numerous categories of new journalists are some who seek to make a significant news event or situation meaningful by describing it minutely (as novelist Truman Capote did with his book on a Nebraska murder case, *In Cold Blood*), or by using some of the devices of the fiction writer (as Gay Talese did in depicting the inner workings of a great newspaper in *The Kingdom and the Power*).

Other branches of new journalism rely on stylistic devices and emotional shadings to invest news with meaning (Tom Wolfe and Jimmy Breslin). Still others draw upon the tools of social science to improve reporting methods and sharpen the clarity of the news account. (Philip Meyer's *Precision Journalism* is a guidebook for this group.)

There is also the category of new journalists, sometimes labeled advocacy journalists or alternative journalists, who have a particular interest in the value-transmission function of the news media and who would like to bring about a significant change in that function. Among those who would likely classify themselves as advocacy or alternative journalists are author Norman Mailer; Bruce Bruggman, who edits a small newspaper in the San Francisco area, *The Bay Guardian;* and Nicholas von Hoffman, the nationally syndicated columnist.

In varying degrees, these and others in the group of advocacy or alternative journalists have taken note of the long-standing tendency of the news media to support the status quo. They believe that this tendency has led all elements of the press to uphold existing power and privilege and to oppose reforms that would benefit large numbers of Americans who are in various ways disadvantaged. What the advocacy journalists would like to do is make the pendulum of the media swing to the other side. They want to wield the power of the media as a deliberate force for change, for what in their judgment would be the betterment of society.

It is worth singling out the followers of this movement for special notice because, should their viewpoint prevail, the value-transmission function of the media would undergo some basic changes. The news media would become less supportive of things as they are; they would be marshalled in support of change, perhaps even of the fundamental changes heretofore considered beyond the limits by most journalists. The media would pay less attention to the ideal of objectivity, tailoring their coverage of the news instead to support what the new journalists regard as desirable change.

Whether the acceptance of such a philosophy by journalists generally would be a good or a bad development depends on the viewpoint of the person making the judgment call. My own conclusions are (1) that the owners and managers of the media will have a good deal to say about how much the performance of the media may be altered by the influence of the advocacy journalists; and (2) that most journalists will very likely continue to see the gatekeeper role, with its adherence to the concept of objectivity as an ideal, as better matched to their perception of the journalistic ethic than would be the advocacy role. But perhaps all that says is that I am of the traditionalist school.

SUMMARY

This chapter has been concerned with the functions of the media as social scientists have defined them: the media as sentinel, scanning the horizon to bring us bulletins of approaching problems or opportunities; the media as organizers of environmental confusion, sorting out relative significance and fitting issues and events into proper relationship; and the media as transmitters of cultural values and standards.

In performing these roles, the news media are affected by such mechanical factors as limitations of space and time, and also by the tendency of journalists to be more proficient and more sure-footed in reporting events that are dramatic and uncomplicated than they are when confronted by complex, far-reaching developments that are difficult both to understand and to report.

We have noted the tendency of some of the news media to emphasize news the public appears to want ahead of news the public needs. We have explored the internal debate among news media people centered on the issue of objectivity and advocacy. And we have examined briefly the paradoxical dual roles of the media as upholders of things as they are, yet channels for the dissemination of changes in social values and practices.

In this section of the book, and in chapter 8 particularly, the approach has been more philosophic than specific. In the next chapter the focus will narrow, to permit examination of some points of direct media-consumer interchange.

9
Media-Consumer Interaction

The relationship between the news media and their consumers is much of the time a one-way affair. The term "mass communication" means a one-to-many flow, and by the nature of the media the "many" have infrequent opportunities to talk back to or apply leverage to the vast enterprises that supply them with tidings of the larger world.

Infrequent as they are, however, the occasions for the equivalent of face-to-face confrontation between consumers and media are worth identifying and evaluating. Some have few significant consequences; but others result either directly or indirectly in important shaping of the news, and thus may fairly be included among the factors that make the media tick.

Let's look first at the matter of feedback in the several media, and then examine in detail various situations in which media actions impinge on the rights of individual consumers and sometimes provoke aggrieved persons to enlist the third-party intervention of the courts.

TALKING BACK

In the case of the broadcast media, consumer feedback is institutionalized and regularly monitored. We noted earlier the audience measurement systems and the life-and-death power their ratings have over television entertainment programs. The ratings help determine the nature of broadcast news, too, as the "happy talk" phenomenon attests.

Of course, the ratings are not individual feedback. They are derived from the reactions of tiny samples of viewers, drawn from the population as a whole in a way that is designed to reflect the preferences of the entire viewing audience. However, an individual with an urge to talk back to the television network or to the local station does have some recourse. The fairness doctrine and the equal time doctrine promulgated by the Federal Communications Commission require that a broadcast outlet provide an opportunity for rejoinder or rebuttal under certain circumstances. The fairness doctrine decrees that if an individual or a cause has been attacked on the air, the broadcaster must provide the attacked entity with a chance to set the record straight, or to fight back. The equal time doctrine assures politicians that if a station makes available to one candidate for office a block of air time to campaign, it must afford similar blocks to other candidates seeking the same office.

These doctrines apply only in the special circumstances described. In addition, some broadcast outlets provide regular opportunities for listener or viewer feedback in the form of talk shows that accept calls from the public. Even a few network news shows provide a limited slot for the equivalent of the newspapers' letters to the editor. On the network, however, the opportunity is severely limited; perhaps four or five viewer reactions a week may be screened on a program viewed by 15 or 20 million persons. The chances for any individual to get in his or her two cents' worth are minuscule.

One other avenue through which consumers can affect broadcast outlets is rarely used. Every television and radio station in the country must seek renewal of its license to operate at three-year intervals. Prior to renewal time, the station must solicit comments of viewers and listeners, keeping files of such comments open to inspection by the public and by representatives of the licensing agency, the Federal Communications Commission.

In the case of most stations the renewal procedures are perfunctory; the FCC considers 8,000 renewal cases every three years, which means that they must be processed at the rate of 10 a day. Obviously, most are *pro forma* matters. But if there are complaints from the public about how a given station discharges its programming and public service responsibilities, the FCC will take a more searching look at that case. The station could lose its license to operate (though this has happened only infrequently). Thus viewers and listeners have a triennial opportunity to exert direct and meaningful influence on the broadcast media, however out of reach those media may seem to be the rest of the time. Most listeners and viewers are probably not aware of this recourse available to them; at any rate, few take advantage of it.

The print media, of course, are not licensed, nor are they subject to the fairness and equal time doctrines. But virtually all of them provide at least some space for reader feedback. All newspapers and most magazines publish letters to the editor. Generally speaking, the smaller the publication, the more accessible is its letters column to the readers. The community newspaper or small-city daily may have space enough to print nearly all the letters it receives, so long as they do not injure individuals or otherwise violate the law. The larger the newspaper, the smaller the percentage of letters received that can be accommodated in print. The very largest papers may be able to publish only 5 percent of the letters, and general circulation magazines find space for an even smaller fraction of reader contributions.

The views expressed in letters to the editor are often closely scrutinized by conscientious editors, and thus sometimes are effective in shaping the news policies of such publications. In editorial offices where ethical scruples are in short supply, however, letters may not only be ignored but may also be so harshly treated by the editor's pencil that other, prospective letter writers may be dissuaded from making the effort.

For example, an unscrupulous editor may use the space argument (a legitimate one) to justify cutting the heart out of a reader's letter. Or he may add a sarcastic editor's note at the end of the letter. Or he may attempt to stack the decks by printing disproportionate percentages of pro and con letters received on a controversial topic, so that public reaction appears to be very different from the mood reflected in the actual flow of letters.

When readers sense that this sort of hatchet job is being performed on their contributions, they understandably lose interest in attempting to provide feedback, and the letters section becomes a flabby repository for thank-you communications and crank letters on oddball topics.

Most editors, however, consistently try to be fair with their correspondents. Letters may have to be cut somewhat to fit space limitations, but the editor makes sure that the trimming leaves each writer's line of argument intact. Precautions are taken that the signature on the letter is authentic, and not a forgery by someone trying to embarrass the supposed letter writer. Editors' notes at the end of letters usually deal only with correction of factual errors in the letters, and do not argue with the writer or insert a derisive last word. And the pro–con breakdown of letters received during a local controversy is reflected in the representative communications that are printed.

Another form of reader feedback—the request for correction of errors that crop up in news stories—is not always treated as responsively and fairly as are letters to the editor. Ideally, when a publication makes a mistake, the mistake should be acknowledged and set right as soon as possible. The correction should match in prominence the original error. That is no more than ethical and responsible journalism.

Some papers make an earnest effort to meet this obligation. The *Wall Street Journal* runs a regular daily feature in the first section, "Corrections and Amplifications," in which any factual or interpretive errors of the previous day's issue are noted and set right. Other papers have adopted the practice, particularly since the mid-1970s.

Yet no one likes to be caught in a mistake. Newspapers particularly shrink from acquiring the reputation of being error-prone. So there is a tendency, both long-standing and widespread, for many newspapers to tuck corrections in as unobtrusively as possible. If a mistake appears on the front page, the correction often shows up several days later next to the classified ads. Moreover, the correction may appear under a headline that fails to tie it effectively to the original story, so that the chances of mending the error are reduced still further.

Not long ago in a newspaper in a college town I saw a lengthy story with a five-column headline. The story was accurate, but the headline was totally misleading and put the college president in a most unfavorable light. I watched for the correction, which came in the next day's paper. But whereas the original story had been 16 column inches in length and displayed under a five-column headline in large type, the correction took up 1½ inches of type under a tiny headline that did not connect the second story to the first. Moreover, the correction appeared on page 6F—that is, deep in the sixth section of the paper—and the original story had been much closer to the front.

As a practical matter the newspaper could not have run the correction in exactly the same form as the original error—as a five-column headline. But the item could have been boxed to gain attention; it could have appeared on the same front-section page that had carried the original story; and the head on the correction could have referred specifically to the original story. Not all the damage could have been undone, since explanations and second versions never quite erase the injury inflicted by an original slur or mistake; but at least the paper would have made a good-faith effort.

Far too many newspapers do not make a good-faith effort on corrections. Some editors even admit that they try to talk complainers out of demanding corrections, or that they deliberately disguise correction stories so that hardly anyone can recognize them; that way they can contend that a correction was run and be technically accurate. But they will not have met their journalistic obligation.

Many observers of the press feel that editors make a serious misjudgment when they opt for a policy of minimizing corrections to avoid the appearance of being error-prone. Each instance of error that is mishandled by an inadequate correction policy very likely makes a permanent enemy in the community. The aggrieved reader will be sure to tell anyone who will listen how shabbily he or she has been treated, and how generally untrustworthy the publication has shown itself to be. A policy of honestly owning up to mistakes and providing adequate corrections will in the long run benefit the publication far more than an automatic cover-up attitude.

WHEN CONSUMERS ARE WRONGED

Certain actions of the news media occasionally injure the sensibilities or the rights of consumers more seriously than does a headline error or a mistreated letter to the editor. In some such instances the injured parties may turn to the law and the courts for help. For, despite all that has been said earlier in this book about the iron-clad protection provided to the media by the First Amendment, the journalist is not above the law if his or her activities invade the rights of other individuals.

The First Amendment was added to the Constitution to ensure that government would not harass the press or interfere with the right of the press to publish freely. This does *not* mean that the press was thus rendered immune from liability for the consequences of publication *after the fact of publication,* if the effect of the publication is to damage the rights of individuals.

To protect the rights of individuals from willful abuse by the news media, each of the 50 states has adopted libel laws that provide a means of redress to persons who have been significantly injured by the actions of the media, either print or broadcast. The direct media-consumer interactions that occur when libel actions are brought must be considered important influences on the way news is covered, and thus very decidedly one of the factors that make the media tick.

The subject of libel law is complex, yet it should be included, at least in summary fashion, in this inventory of the forces that influence the shape of the news. Whether you are interested in the functioning of the media as a prospective practitioner or simply with the aim of becoming a more informed and discriminating consumer of media products, you should have some understanding of what the laws of libel can and cannot do to safeguard individual rights and curb the power of the press.

Libel law is entirely in the form of state statutes and common law; there is no federal law of libel. Second, although there are criminal libel statutes, they are seldom invoked; almost all libel suits are civil actions—that is, between one private party and another (one of which is a publication, a broadcaster, or an individual who has disseminated information in some fashion).

In the simplest terms, libel law rests on the assumption that any of us has an inherent right to be secure in the reputation established by our deeds and words. If that good name and reputation are taken away or badly marred by the effect of a publication of any kind, we are entitled to seek recompense from the courts under the laws of libel.

If you are called a thief, a murderer, or a liar in published or broadcast material, you should be entitled to go to court to have your good name restored, your reputation "made whole" again. If in some published material you are accused unwarrantedly of unfair business practices, or unethical professional dealings, you should have the right to collect damages from the disseminator of the libel. If a publication, a picture, a cartoon, or a broadcast makes you out a figure of ridicule and causes persons in your community to think less of you, you should be entitled to seek a libel judgment and an award of damages.

Through the years, the courts have interpreted some key terms in libel law in a very broad sense. Thus "publication" doesn't mean only an article in a newspaper. It also means a television or radio broadcast, a campaign flier tacked up on telephone poles all over town, a form letter sent to numbers of people, a headline, a picture, or an advertisement.

To establish that you have been injured by some form of libelous publication, you need not be able to prove that the whole town knows about it and that as a result you are being shunned on the streets. All you need to establish is that a "substantial number" of right-thinking persons gained a bad impression of you from the published material. What this means in precise terms is up to an individual judge or jury, but it has been held to mean as few as half a dozen persons.

If you have been injured by some form of libelous publication and if you take your case to court and win a jury verdict, your wounded feelings may be salved by a damage award in the form of a cash payment. Depending upon the severity of the injury to your reputation, or the degree to which your business or professional activities have suffered, the award may range from a few hundred dollars to as much as a million. The legal entity responsible for disseminating the libelous publication must pay this award, unless an appellate court modifies the award or reverses the verdict for some reason.

SOME LOOPHOLES

On the basis of the foregoing explanation of the workings of the law of libel, you would be justified in assuming that it is a bonanza for media consumers, a foolproof way to get back at the mighty news machines that can affect our lives so swiftly and disastrously.

But there's a catch. Several, in fact.

The same libel laws whose main purpose is the protection of the rights of individuals also must take into account the obligation and right of the media to publish freely the news that the public needs to have to keep our representative democracy functioning. In other words, the libel laws have been drafted so as to walk a fine line. They are intended to protect individuals from media abuse; but they are also drawn so as to prevent frivolous harassment of the press, and to ensure that the press will not be handcuffed in its role of proxy for the people, keeping a watchful eye on the workings of government and governors.

Thus the libel laws provide several important exceptions (or loopholes, depending on your viewpoint) designed to limit media liability. These exceptions (or loopholes) have been structured in the form of defenses that lawyers representing a news medium may interpose to defeat a plaintiff's attempt to win a damage verdict.

A number of such defenses are recognized in various state libel laws, but only three are universal and frequently invoked. They are the defense of *truth*, the defense of *privilege*, and the defense of *fair comment and criticism*.

Truth

If the lawyers representing the newspaper or broadcaster you are suing can show that what was published about you was in all significant respects "substantially" true, and not published maliciously with a deliberate intent to hurt you, you probably will lose your case. For example, if the local newspaper refers to you as a liar, and then can provide evidence in court that you have indeed played fast and loose with the facts, the judge and jury will probably rule that your reputation has been damaged by your own actions, not by the publication.

The defense of truth protects news media that uncover evidence of crime or corruption, for example, or expose unsanitary conditions in a food-processing plant, or call attention to the operation of a bunco gang. It helps to discourage the filing of nuisance suits by persons who really are as they have been described in the media, but hope to throw up such a smoke screen of protest that the public will think they have been wronged.

Privilege

The defense of privilege derives from the thesis that records of the public business and activities of those elected or appointed to conduct the public business ought to be available to the press so that they can be reported to the public. How else would the public be able to learn how honestly and effectively its business was being conducted by those given temporary stewardship? From that thesis has developed the argument that the press ought to be free to publish records of official business without fear that those records might include libelous material. Thus the transcripts of public and official proceedings (trials, for example, or debates in Congress, or testimony taken by such a body as the select congressional committee to investigate the Watergate affair) are considered to be privileged. If there is libelous material in those records, and that material is *accurately* published in the news media, those media are deemed to be protected in that publication, and the aggrieved parties cannot hope for successful recourse in the libel laws. The defense of privilege may be invoked, however, only in the case of *official* and *public* records and proceedings. (Thus an executive session of a congressional committee, to which the public is not admitted, would not be a privileged proceeding; it is official, but not public. The same is true of a grand jury session, which is not open to the public.)

The purpose of the defense of privilege is to ensure that the news media are not deterred from their essential function of serving the public's need to know about the conduct of public business.

Note that the defense of privilege is based on *reflected* privilege, since it attaches only to records and actions that are themselves privileged. Members of Congress acting in their official capacities on the floor of the House or Senate in open session have under the Constitution an absolute privilege; that is, they cannot be called to account in a civil court for anything they may say in that setting, even if what they say may be libelous of someone. Because it acts for the public in reporting the debates of the Congress, the press shares in part in this absolute privilege, but *only* to the extent that it gives a full and fair report of public and official actions. Thus a newspaper can report the libelous comments of a congressman if he makes those comments in the course of House debate. But if the same congressman had made the same libelous comments not in the House but during a speech to the Washington Chamber of Commerce, he would not have been in a privileged situation. (The occasion was public, to be sure, but not official.) And if the press had reported the luncheon speech libel, both the newspapers and the congressman would be accountable in the courts; the defense of privilege would be futile.

Journalists rely on the defense of privilege to protect them only when they are reporting from public and official records, or when they are covering public officials acting in their official capacity, as defined by the Constitution and the laws.

Fair Comment and Criticism

For generations the defense of fair comment and criticism was narrow and specialized, applicable only in certain types of cases. In recent years, however, it has been interpreted much more broadly, and has become one of the most effective shields available to the news media when they become targets of libel actions.

Originally, the defense of fair comment and criticism could be called upon only in situations where a publication had expressed an opinion about the activities of persons (such as artists, writers, or politicians) who had voluntarily invited public approval of those activities. An actor who performed in a play, an author who published a book, or a person who ran for office was considered to have solicited the approval of the public in the form of attendance at the play, purchase of the book, or polling-booth support for the office-seeker. Thus the quality of the actor's performance or the author's book, and the qualifications for office of the politician, were considered to be matters the public needed to know about to decide whether to attend the play, buy the book, or vote for the candidate. The press was considered to have a right to provide the public with opinions on these points; if those opinions were harsh and derogatory and the object of the criticism understandably took umbrage, he or she just had to grin and bear it. After all, the critical evaluation had been invited when the artistic effort or the political qualifications of the aggrieved person had been set before the public, and the monetary or ballot-box support of the public solicited.

As it initially took form through statute and case law, the defense of fair comment and criticism was strictly limited to expressions of opinion. It was equally limited to that special area of artistic effort or personal qualification for which public approval had been voluntarily sought. If material purported to be factual rather than opinion were contained in the publication, or if the publication dealt with anything about the subject that did not have to do with the "performance-related" activities or characteristics of the subject, the defense of fair comment and criticism would not apply.

Thus a reviewer could observe that an author's book was "an empty, pedestrian, repetitive, worthless compendium of junk" and the defense of fair comment would provide a buffer against a libel action. But if the reviewer went on to say that "little else could be expected from a man who peddles hard drugs on the side and has been an international lecher for years," the author could sue for the damage the latter observation had inflicted on his personal (not literary) reputation, and the publication would have to find some defense other than fair comment and criticism if it hoped to escape damages.

The implications of the fair comment and criticism defense were generally clear-cut so far as actors, authors, and other artists were concerned. But you can see that in the case of politicians, drawing the line between "performance-related" activities or characteristics, and aspects of private life or personality, might be difficult. Whether an author is a chronic alcoholic may be totally unrelated to the quality of his writing; on the other hand, if a chronic alcoholic is seeking public office, is his alcoholism something to be weighed publicly along with his conventional qualifications for office, or is it outside the bounds of fair comment and criticism?

Questions like these were at least partially answered by a momentous series of Supreme Court decisions that began with *New York Times Co.* v. *Sullivan* in 1964. The effect of these decisions was to establish a new line of defense against libel actions brought by individuals who were public officials or could be considered "public persons."

In *Times* v. *Sullivan* the Court held that the First Amendment guarantee of freedom of the press meant that the press should be able to maintain an uninhibited, "robust," wide-open debate on public affairs. Such a debate, said the Court, would inevitably involve some erroneous and defamatory publications. But if such defamatory errors were published *without actual malice,* injured parties who were public officials or public figures should not be able to collect damages from the offending publications, lest this inhibit the robust debate called for by the Court's constitutional interpretation. "Actual malice" the Court defined as prior knowledge that the published material was false, or "reckless disregard" of whether it was false.

The initial 1964 decision made the new constitutional defense applicable to persons actually holding public office. (In *Times* v. *Sullivan* the official was the police commissioner of Montgomery, Alabama.) Subsequent decisions successively broadened the scope of the original ruling, including more and more categories of persons among those to whom the defense might apply. One such decision extended the *Times* v. *Sullivan* doctrine to persons who were not public officials at the time of the publication, but had at one time held some government office. (Retired Major General Edwin Walker was the figure in that case.) Next the Court applied the 1964 ruling to "public figures," persons who had never held any government position but who had by their activities involved themselves significantly in public affairs. (Syndicated columnist Drew Pearson, who commented regularly on national affairs, and Linus Pauling, a scientist who had lent his name in support of various special interest groups active in politics, are examples.) Finally, one case applied the *Times* v. *Sullivan* doctrine to a New York City policeman—not a chief, a captain, or even a sergeant, but a simple patrolman on the beat.

In the eyes of some observers of the press the Court's expanding doctrine had grown too sweeping. The press did, indeed, need freedom to comment on public affairs and public figures. But did it need such wide freedom? Were the protections of the libel law being stripped from too many categories of persons? Persons both inside and outside the media worried that the reduction of libel restraints on the press regarding public officials and "public figures" would lead to such excesses of attack and criticism that public opinion would be aroused and a climate established in which dangerously rigid limitations on the press might be advocated and even adopted.

Recent Supreme Court decisions, perhaps responding to this concern, have swung the pendulum back somewhat and modified the categories of "public figures." But the new constitutional defense against libel remains strong, and press commentary on politicians in particular continues to be "robust."

The existence of libel laws and the recourse to them by injured individuals from time to time importantly influence how the news media perform. The possibility of having to face a libel action if a certain story is published may inhibit a city editor from giving the go-ahead. Libel actions are very expensive, even if the case is eventually won at some appellate level. Lawyers and others who recognize this have used the threat of legal action to stall or divert press exposés. Many a libel action has been filed by persons who never intend to press the matter to trial. They hope that by filing the suit and demanding extravagant damages (some plaintiffs have sought as much as $10,000,000), they will accomplish twin ends: the publication will be rendered cautious and timid about taking any further pokes at the plaintiff, and the public will assume that the plaintiff must have been truly wronged and must have an airtight case to ask such astronomical damages. Thus at one stroke the plaintiff can tie the pesky medium's hands for a time and also achieve a fair degree of rehabilitation in the public eye. That the case may never be tried is not likely to be noticed a year or so hence, when the court docket might be expected to have room for it.

Basically, however, the libel laws are a necessary protection for the rights of individuals who in some fashion are badly used by the media. The media are so powerful and can wreak such damage on individual lives and reputations that the ordinary consumer needs a helping hand from the law and the courts when his or her good name is besmirched unwarrantedly by one of the news media.

In virtually all situations, the press can do its job effectively within the reasonable limitations imposed by the laws of libel. They are a modest price for the preservation of individual rights in this era of vast media enterprises with incalculable power to do good or ill.

INVASION OF PRIVACY

Another form of recourse is available to the consumer in situations in which the media abuse their power by intruding needlessly and harmfully on the privacy of individuals.

There are statutes that deal with media invasion of individual privacy just as the laws of libel deal with damage to reputations, but privacy laws aren't as universal as libel laws. Much of the law involving invasion of privacy is case law—that is, law built gradually on the basis of precedent decisions reached in cases litigated through the years. However, there is a spreading tendency to embody such case law in statutes in more and more states.

Invasion of privacy cases arise when someone is given media exposure that he or she didn't want and perhaps didn't deserve. Instances have involved individuals whose pictures were used for advertising purposes without their consent, and other persons who were thrust into a news situation and thus made unwilling targets of media attention. Court actions have dealt with such widely differing situations as that of a woman who sued for invasion of privacy when a newspaper published a picture of her going through a carnival fun-house just as a concealed stream of air blew her skirts up around her; and the case of a family whose ordeal as hostages of a group of gunmen was later made into a television program that brought a revival of all the terrible memories and a renewal of unwelcome publicity.

Invasion of privacy cases have also arisen when the news media discovered something in the distant past of someone in the community and exploited the discovery for current news purposes, to the embarrassment or injury of the individual involved.

Invasion of privacy cases are now and then won by the aggrieved party, but not so frequently as in the field of libel. The ground rules are much more complicated.

When is a person legitimately a subject of news coverage, whether or not that coverage represents an intrusion on privacy? Can someone photographed while lying injured beside an auto wreck successfully press a claim for invasion of privacy? The courts have typically ruled that in such a situation the individual has become part of the news and thus cannot object to being depicted, whether in words or in pictures.

Can a person who is photographed incidentally in a crowd scene at a sports event (when he was supposed to be at a business appointment) contend that his privacy has been invaded and that he has lost his job as a consequence of his picture having appeared on the sports page? In one such case the court ruled that the man did have a cause of action.

Consider a somewhat more complex and consequential case. On September 22, 1975, President Gerald Ford emerged from the St. Francis Hotel in San Francisco to find a crowd waiting to greet him. As the president moved through the crowd, a woman drew a revolver from her purse and aimed it directly at the president from a few feet away. A man standing near her saw the action and struck her arm just as she fired, deflecting the shot and possibly saving Ford's life.

Several days later a *San Francisco Chronicle* columnist published a report suggesting that the man, a former Marine, was a homosexual. Later, other papers and the wire services picked up the report and published it around the country. The man said that the publicity had made his relatives aware of his sexual orientation for the first time and contended that his life had been ruined. He sued for invasion of privacy.

The case is still pending as this is written, so its legal merits cannot properly be discussed. But the questions involved are complicated and difficult to resolve. Had the man, by his action, thrust himself into the news and thus made himself a legitimate subject for press attention? Could such press attention properly extend to exploration of the man's personal life and characteristics? How far can the news media appropriately go in satisfying public curiosity about persons who for one reason or another suddenly become newsworthy? Presumably the courts will eventually provide some answers, if the case is brought to trial.

Various kinds of media intrusion upon the privacy of individuals do not fall within the purview of the courts because they do not involve alleged or actual violations of the law. Yet they perplex conscientious journalists and may be of painful significance to the individuals involved. The factors that determine how the news media deal with such borderline cases are among the matters we should consider in exploring how the news media tick.

QUESTIONS OF ETHICS

Virtually every day the women and men who gather the news and process it for dissemination to the public through one of the mass media face trying decisions involving not legal but ethical considerations.

The reporter covering the story of a fire in a rooming house must decide what details to include in his account; the photographer at an accident scene must pick the subjects and the camera angles; the videotape editor must decide whether to cut an unintentional blooper out of an interview or to let it run. The values to be weighed in all these decisions involve more than newsworthiness, although that is always a prominent consideration in any journalistic situation. There is also the factor of human sensitivities—the sensitivities of those who are caught up, perhaps inadvertently, in the news itself, and the sensitivities of others whose lives may be affected by the way the story is handled.

Many press critics automatically assume that close decisions in news situations are always or usually made on the basis of what will make the most dramatic story or the most arresting TV footage. That is very often not the case. Most journalists are aware that their work can profoundly affect the dignity and the lives of persons who become part of the news. They try to take human values as well as journalistic values into account in their decisions.

Bill Moyers, who has been both a print and TV journalist, observed:

> While I know it is admirable to be cool and detached and even-handed about the human scene we describe on the air or in print, I find it impossible to be unconcerned about the fate of the actors on the stage. For they're not really actors, not merely characters in a play who will assume another role when the curtain has come down and the audience and the critics have gone home. Thieves and victims, Presidents and press secretaries, labor chieftains and protesters in the street, drug peddlers and drug addicts, mothers on welfare, auto workers out of work, hookers and movie stars alike, secretaries of state and peasants huddling in the ruins of a Cambodian village all have something very basic in common: we're all pilgrims on the same journey. Some may be up to more mischief than others. Some may be brighter, and some may be blinder. Some may be luckier and others tragically miscast through no fault of their own. But we are all cousins of the same family and the same end awaits us all. . . . Journalists are human. . . .[18]

The journalist on the razor edge of a decision between newsworthiness on the one hand and individual sensitivities on the other is in an uncomfortable position. Most newspeople probably share Moyers's humane concern for the temporary "actors" on the journalistic stage; yet they also have an obligation to report the news so that the public will be informed. In the process they face many tough judgment calls.

Let's look at a few actual cases on which editors and reporters held honest differences of opinion about the right way to act. Consider, as you read, what *your* decision might have been in the same circumstances. In the process you should gain some insight into how the nature of the news is sometimes determined.

Case 1

A photographer assigned to an accident story arrived on the scene as the fatally injured driver was being taken away by ambulance. The wrecked car was still in place on the street. Just then the mother of the injured boy arrived

and at once broke down in grief. The photographer, standing in front of the de-
molished car, took one dramatic shot. It was framed by the wreckage of the
windshield and body of the car, and behind the car, peering into the back
window, was visible the stricken mother, her face twisted with agony, her
mouth open in a soundless cry. The picture editor of the newspaper played this
shot four columns wide across the top of page one. The caption read: ''A
shocked mother stares at wreckage she came across . . . today just after her
17-year-old son, fatally injured, was taken away by ambulance.''

In the days that followed, the newspaper received numerous letters to the
editor, virtually all critical of the use of the picture. Some sample excerpts,
with names and locales omitted unless they are essential to the meaning:

> It is very shocking that this picture . . . can be condoned as an excellent
> piece of photojournalism. . . . May God have mercy on you. . . .

> I have never seen anything so disgusting in my life. . . . Would you want a tragic
> moment in your life plastered on a front page for thousands to see? Will it stop
> here or will you send your photographers into hospitals and funeral homes to
> ''candidly'' catch people in sorrow at the very personal time of a death? . . .

> I was outraged at the . . . front page photo of a mother's anguish when she
> came upon the scene of her son's fatal accident. . . . These stories are news, but
> they can be told without exploiting human misery. I deplore this kind of
> photojournalism.

> We are curious as to the motives and rationale behind the public
> presentation of an obviously personal and hopefully private moment of human
> emotion. Who is gaining from such capitalization on an honest expression of grief
> and suffering? . . . It would seem that such a photograph inappropriately
> displayed on the front page of a newspaper would appeal to the very small portion
> of your readership who have an obscene and obsessive interest in human
> suffering. . . .

The photographer, the picture editor, and other decision makers on the
paper defended the use of the picture, citing its powerful impact. They
suggested that such pictures serve as a warning to others and may prevent other
mishaps.

Where lay the right? Certainly the journalists involved were correct in
their assessment of the newsworthiness of the picture; it later won an award
in a photojournalism competition. Yet didn't the readers who complained
also have a valid point? The wreck could have been shown without the mother's tortured face captured within its frame, and still have served as a warning. Was the paper encouraging a morbid voyeurism on the part of its readers
by publishing the picture? Was the newsworthiness of the photograph so arrest-

ing that it outweighed the injury done to the sensitivities of the mother and other members of the dead boy's family?

Accident pictures appear in the newspapers and on television screens regularly. Their impact is undeniable. Their merit as news is arguable, depending on your definition of news. Making the decision to use, or not to use, such shots can be an ordeal for a journalist who shares Moyers's conviction that human sensibilities should weigh on the scales as well as considerations of newsworthiness and the public's right to know.

Case 2

This case involves an Associated Press wirephoto published in a West Coast metropolitan daily. At one side of the picture was a woman, her face displaying both anguish and entreaty, one hand stretched toward a policeman on the other side of the picture. The policeman wore an expression of compassion, and also had one hand stretched toward the woman, as though to restrain her. The caption under the picture read: "Pleads to see son's body. _____ _____, whose 10-year-old son was found slain Thursday, pleads with police officer in Trenton, N.J., to let her see the body. Police said the body was found nude and beaten in an alley."

The auto accident picture discussed in case 1 could in some respects be defended as having a wholesome warning effect on others. It is difficult to make such a case for the photograph of the mother and the policeman. Moreover, since it dealt with an incident that took place across the continent from the location of the newspaper that published the picture, its newsworthiness for local readers seems to depend more on shock value and morbid curiosity than anything else. Yet it was published, four columns wide. How would you have decided?

Case 3

A strike was underway in a large East Coast city. It had tied up one of the region's largest industrial plants, proving costly to workers and management alike. Into the office of the local paper one day came two lawyers representing the ownership of the struck company. One of the lawyers was also a member of the board of directors of the newspaper. The two lawyers informed the editor of the paper that the leader of the strike had formerly been a member of the Communist party; they felt the newspaper should publicize this, since it might disillusion the strikers and lead to an end of the walkout that was so destructive of the local economy.

The editors investigated and discovered that the union leader had indeed been a card-carrying Communist some 20 years earlier. There was no evidence, however, that his membership had continued or that he still held similar views.

The editors decided not to use the story, on the ground that the man's distant background was not relevant to the current situation and that there was no justification for compromising his leadership position with his union. They stuck to the decision despite pressure from the company and from ownership, and the strike wound down eventually to a negotiated settlement.

Were they right to consider the reputation and rights of the union leader, when they had at hand an opportunity to break a strike that was crippling the community? Did the public have a right to know that the man who was leading the strike had a Communist background? Where would you have come down on the matter had you been in the editor's chair, with a member of your board of directors sitting scross the desk?

Case 4

Back, once more, to pictures.

On November 12, 1975, Supreme Court Justice William O. Douglas announced that illness compelled him to retire from the seat he had occupied on the highest court in the land longer than any other justice in history.

Numerous pictures moved on the wire services that day and the next. One that was widely used showed Justice Douglas in the wheelchair to which he had been confined for some months after suffering a stroke. His young wife was leaning over him. The judge's frailty could be discerned in his gaunt features. The caption read: "Associate Supreme Court Justice William O. Douglas and Mrs. Douglas chat with newsmen at their Washington, D.C., home Wednesday night following the announcement of his retirement from the court earlier in the day. Douglas served nearly 37 years on the court, longer than any other justice."

Among the other pictures on the wires the next morning was an enlarged close-up of Justice Douglas; only his head was in the picture. His face clearly showed a two-day stubble of beard; his eyes were wide and staring. He was scarcely recognizable and could easily have been taken for a skid road wino. The caption: "William O. Douglas, 77, in photo taken as he left his home this morning, the day after he announced his retirement from the Supreme Court."

Not many newspapers that I saw used that photograph, but one did—five columns wide by eight inches deep, on page one.

For what purpose do you suppose the editors chose to use that picture? The earlier wheelchair photo was sufficiently revealing of the physical condition of the distinguished jurist, providing a possibly newsworthy explanation for his decision to retire. The close-up head shot, spread over five columns, added nothing of news value. It *did*, however, portray the ill and aging justice at his worst; it was a cruel portrait to leave with the public as perhaps the last glimpse of one of the most significant legal figures of the era. That's my personal judgment, of course. Obviously, at least some editors didn't agree with it.

Case 5

The *Dallas Times-Herald* uncovered a story that a 69-year-old retired oil engineer had been at one time a Soviet spy and then later an FBI double-agent. The man involved acknowledged the accuracy of the story, but repeatedly asked that it not be used. At the time publication was imminent he warned that he would kill himself if the story was run. The paper's editors decided to go ahead with publication, and the man did indeed kill himself the day after the story appeared.

The *Times-Herald* executive editor who made the final decision on whether to use the story, Ken Johnson, told *Newsweek* that news-papers occasionally receive threats about stories from people attempting to protect their identities. If a story is newsworthy and supported by the facts, however, it is the paper's policy to publish.[19] Most of Johnson's fellow editors around the country supported the decision, saying they would have acted simi-larly. Elie Abel, dean of the Columbia University Graduate School of Journal-ism, observed of the case that the hardest problem is how compassionate a re-porter can be and still do his or her job.[20]

What would you have done in Johnson's shoes? Suppress the story? Hold back until the man could have been placed under psychiatric care? Run it as written?

Case 6

In early 1975 a Belleville, Illinois, 14-year-old named Heidi Biggs was dying of cancer. She had expressed a wish to visit Hawaii before she died. Hearing of this, a Canadian businessman raised funds to make the trip pos-sible. Heidi and her mother flew to Honolulu for what was to be a two-week stay.

Stories similar to this crop up in the news every so often. Usually they are covered sympathetically and briefly as human interest episodes. Not so with Heidi's journey to Hawaii.

Every day that she was in the islands the Honolulu papers ran pictures and stories on the dying girl and her trip. There were photos of Heidi and her mother arriving and being decked with flower leis. There were later pictures of Heidi having one last ride on a horse, sitting on the beach, and visiting cele-brated sights in Honolulu. Daily news stories carried such headlines as HEIDI SUFFERS BAD MORNING, BUT RECOVERS; HEIDI'S STEPDAD TO JOIN HER HAWAII "DREAM TRIP"; STEPDAD ARRIVES TO SEE HEIDI AT HOSPITAL; HER CANA-DIAN BENEFACTOR HERE FOR VISIT WITH HEIDI. (The last two stories were ac-companied by emotional photographs, one of the step-father embracing the bald, wasted girl in her hospital bed—radiation treatments for the cancer had earlier caused all her hair to fall out—and another of the Canadian businessman conversing with Heidi as she lay in the hospital.)

There was a story of her departure from the islands, supported by her mother's arms in the waiting room of the airport, hardly aware of her surroundings by then. And there was the final headline: HEIDI'S JOURNEY ENDS. The story told of her death in an ambulance, 20 minutes after her plane had landed on the trip home from Hawaii.

It was, as United Press International editor Dan Carmichael rightly termed it, a classic instance of press exploitation, "bathetic media coverage . . . ghoulish attempts at self-promotion by Heidi's hosts . . ."—attempts that were media-assisted in some instances.[21]

At least some of the newspeople on the Hawaii newspaper staffs were sickened by the situation. One writer assigned for several days to the Heidi saga finally flatly refused to write any more stories about the girl; others freely admitted their embarrassment at the way in which the plight of a dying child was being exploited for "good copy."

The case seems so extreme and clear-cut that it hardly belongs in this list of close judgment calls. Yet the fact remains that not only the Honolulu media but many on the mainland ran all the Heidi stories and film, day after day, wringing every last tear out of the episode. And millions of readers and viewers avidly absorbed each detail.

In retrospect, the six ethical cases may not appear difficult to decide rightly. Yet remember that the newspersons involved in them had to operate under pressure of deadlines, and within the media context that places great value on newsworthiness. In those circumstances the values may not seem so simple to sort out.

Almost every day, the men and women of the media must make narrowly balanced decisions at every level of the newsgathering and -disseminating system. These are decisions with ethical rather than legal implications, matters of taste and compassion. How such decisions are finally taken, whether on the basis of news values or human values, decides the shape of the news that consumers finally receive.

TWO AMENDMENTS AT ODDS

One other area of press coverage affecting individuals perhaps doesn't fit entirely logically here, since it involves a specialized group of individuals, and it does not deal with direct media-consumer relationships. But it appears to fit better at this point than it might in the other sections of the book. And certainly it offers further insights into how and why the news is shaped.

I am referring to the problems that arise when the media cover news about persons on trial for a crime, or awaiting trial. Such problems are often lumped under the slightly misleading label, "fair trial versus free press."

In covering news of crime and the courts, journalists frequently find themselves walking an indistinct but important line. In such a situation two constitutional amendments of equally fundamental importance to our system of government and society often seem to conflict.

The First Amendment provides that the press shall be free from government interference in its mission of reporting the news to the public. This includes news of how the machinery of law enforcement is functioning—how the police, the prosecutors, the judges, and the juries are carrying out their obligations.

Yet as the media representatives cover the news generated in these areas, they can easily run afoul of another, equally important amendment, the Sixth. This provides that every citizen accused of a crime must be given a prompt, public trial by an unbiased jury of his or her peers. The key word, so far as our present discussion is concerned, is *unbiased*. It can easily happen that the news media covering a criminal case publish material that could contaminate prospective jurors by prejudicing them against a defendant before they ever enter the courtroom and the jury box. That would leave the defendant deprived of one of the protections guaranteed by the Sixth Amendment.

This has been a sticky, unresolved problem for decades. On one side are arrayed the supporters of the press, adamant that the news media must be free to report fully on the activities of the law enforcement machinery. Otherwise, they argue, the public will lack information it must have to reach decisions about the effectiveness of our legal institutions and the probity of those who administer those institutions. Moreover, if the press cannot keep the spotlight of publicity on the workings of the police and court systems, what is to prevent the rights of accused persons from being violated behind the screen of silence? There are, after all, some few judges susceptible to bribery, some police given to brutality—so long as they are confident they won't be found out.

On the other side of the argument are those who point out that a defendant's constitutional rights can be destroyed by excessive press coverage that prevents trial by an unbiased jury. The right of an individual under the Sixth Amendment, they correctly insist, is on a footing with the right of the press under the First; a distinctive keystone of the American system is the safeguarding of individual rights from injury by the collective forces of society.

How, as a practical matter, do instances of this conflict between constitutional rights arise? How can they be resolved equitably?

Most fair trial–free press issues are generated in celebrated criminal cases that, because of the unusual nature of the crime or because of the prominence of the victim or the accused, draw extensive media coverage. This involves only a very small fraction of the total number of criminal cases brought to trial; most criminal cases are covered cursorily or not at all, particularly by the large-circulation media. In a very small community, of course, almost any crime of violence will be given play by the local newspaper or broadcaster.

If in a newsworthy case the newspapers and the broadcast media give extensive coverage to the accused, detailing his capture, listing his previous criminal record, perhaps quoting from confessions made to the police, it will be difficult to impanel in that community a jury of persons who have not been exposed to information that would probably lead them to prejudgments.

Yet when a suspected criminal is at large, shouldn't the public have information about his prior record, which suggests how dangerous he might be? Shouldn't the public be informed when the suspect is caught and charged with the crime? If the news media do not cover the preliminary stages of a criminal case, aren't they defaulting on their obligation to provide the public with news it needs for self-protective reasons, if nothing else?

News media decision makers and newsgatherers alike are keenly aware of the difficult dilemma posed by the clash of constitutional rights in the coverage of news of crime and criminals.

Editors, broadcasters, judges, and attorneys in many states have joined to devise codes for covering news stories of crime without jeopardizing the rights of the accused. Much of the time these codes function reasonably well, but if the case is particularly lurid or involves highly newsworthy principals, the well-meant code provisions may be temporarily forgotten.

When eight nurses were shot to death in a Chicago apartment, when a sniper in a tower at a Texas university campus picked off victims at random, when Jack Ruby fatally shot Lee Harvey Oswald on television as millions watched, when the bodies of two dozen farm workers were found in a California wood—in all these cases and others that you would instantly recall, there was extensive publicity and clear injury to the right of the accused to be tried before a jury of persons who would give an unbiased hearing to the evidence.

Yet it should be noted that cases usually cited by critics of the press tend to be extreme, clearly out of the ordinary. In most instances where press coverage has in some way infringed upon the rights of a defendant, the infringement is on a much less damaging scale. Moreover, in most such cases (not, of course, in a Ruby-Oswald situation) the court can take steps to restore the defendant's rights—by ordering a new trial, by setting aside a verdict, by directing a change of venue (moving the trial to some other locale where there has been less extensive publicity), or by issuing corrective instructions to the jury.

These are resolutions of the fair trial–free press dilemma that both sides to the argument will accept. The press, however, strongly and rightly resists some other remedies that some judges have employed, such as gag orders that seek to bar all press coverage of a case until the jury's verdict has been returned.

It seems likely that the seesaw struggle between press and courts over the relative priorities of the two amendments will continue in some fashion for the indefinite future. Partial remedies have been developed, but until a complete, clear-cut answer is found, the fair trial–free press issue will remain one of the factors that help to shape the news.

SUMMARY

Section 3 has examined the ways in which the relationship of the news media to consumers affects the gathering and reporting of the news.

Much of the time the media and the consumers are at a very long arm's length. The media consumer who is not an advertiser or a news source typically has little or no direct feedback impact on the newspapers, magazines, and broadcast networks.

We also looked at the relationship in terms of theory versus practice: what is it that the scholars and social scientists say the media should be doing for and to the consuming public, and exactly how well are the media doing these things?

Scholars say that the communication media provide a sentinel or watchtower service to the public. They scout the world scene, scan the horizon, and bring us information and ideas from all quarters. We depend upon the media for warnings, for tidings of opportunities, for the human interest accounts that assure us of the universality of human nature.

In carrying out the sentinel function, the media are handicapped by space and time limitations, by craft attitudes and convictions built over years of experience, and by the ubiquitous need to balance the kinds of news and information people *want* (so that the medium will be successful economically) and the kinds of news and information people *need* to survive in our system.

A second function of the news media, according to the scholars, is to order the events that swirl about us in such bewildering, even intimidating fashion. The media help fit these events and personalities or causes into context, so that we can see meaningful patterns and trends rather than a hopeless blur.

As they attempt to carry out this ordering function, the men and women of the media have to rely upon stereotypes. They must also contend with the unending debate over whether news should be (or can be) reported objectively, or from a stance of frank advocacy. The persons who report, process, and present the news may also have problems carrying out the ordering function because they are, as a group, somewhat different in background and outlook from the majority of those in the consuming public. Also, an individual journalist can know only so much, and lack of expertise may limit the usefulness of his or her attempt at explaining the complex and bringing order and meaning to the swollen flow of events.

The third function assigned by the social scientists to the news media—that of transmitting the cultural heritage from one generation to the next—we have largely left to be considered in another volume of this series. It will be devoted entirely to popular culture and the role of the news media as both creators and carriers of cultural values.

We did note, however, the paradox that the media are simultaneously supporters of things as they are, yet channels through which change in society is often accomplished.

In addition to the arm's-length theoretical relationship between the lone consumer and the great news-processing enterprises, there are some kinds of direct, head-to-head contacts between the media and those they serve. We looked at some of those in detail, particularly such instances of contact that brought the power of the media to bear injuriously on the rights of individuals. And we examined the various remedies and recourses, legal and other, available to individuals whose lives have been intruded upon unwarrantedly by the functioning of the media of mass communication.

All of this contributed to an expanded understanding of how the news media tick, and what ideological and practical forces influence the way the news is gathered, packaged, and offered to the eventual consumer.

SECTION FOUR
THE MEDIA
AND
ACCOUNTABILITY

B enjamin Franklin wrote in the very early days of the United States:

> Abuses of the freedom of speech ought to be repressed, but to whom do we dare commit the power of doing it?[1]

In 1815 John Adams observed:

> If there is ever to be an amelioration of the condition of mankind, philosophers, theologians, legislators, politicians and moralists will find that the regulation of the press is the most difficult, dangerous, and important problem they have to solve. Mankind cannot now be governed without it, nor at present with it.[2]

From the days of Franklin and Adams to our own, the dilemma has remained. Anyone with an eye to see and an ear to hear can recognize that the media of mass communication—and the men and women who staff those media, at every level—wield enormous power. That power, as we have noted, can be used to uncover corruption, to protect individual rights, and to expose demagogues. But the same power can also be used by journalists to play God, controlling the nominations and the campaigns of presidential candidates, or deciding whether to destroy the reputation of an individual caught up in some eruption of the news.

Whenever great power is concentrated in the hands of a relatively few persons, the possibility of abuse exists. In many sectors of society controls exist to minimize, at least, the incidence and impact of such abuses. In our federal government a carefully crafted system of checks and balances functions to that end (as it did, finally, in the case of Watergate).

In other sectors of society government itself provides, on authorization of the people, various forms of control. The quality of food sold to the public is regulated, the operations of the stock exchanges are supervised by a government agency, and the rates that utilities can charge for electricity, gas, telephone service, and water are set by instrumentalities of the various states. The power of unions is controlled by laws setting the ground rules for bargaining between management and unions and stipulating the kinds of actions that may be taken to settle disagreements. The power of great corporations is limited by antitrust laws and by requirements for disclosure of financial dealings.

Yet one of the most massive concentrations of power in our society (mightier by far than anything Franklin or Adams dreamed of) is subject to only the flimsiest sort of formal or codified controls—watered-down libel laws, and some statutes limiting the publication of obscenity (which have been substantially vitiated by Supreme Court decisions).

The news media, throughout the nation's history, have been armored in the protections of the First Amendment. These have effectively frustrated the occasional attempt by an exasperated government to impose effective limitations on press freedom (such as the alien and sedition laws, for example, or the prior censorship injunctions sought in the Pentagon Papers case).

No responsible figure, from Franklin's day to this, has suggested that the First Amendment ought to be repealed and the armor of the news media stripped away.

Our government system, our social structure, our individual liberties literally depend for their survival on the continuation of freedom of expression for both people and press. We know that, and so do the media writers, editors, and broadcasters. Yet we also know that the protected power of the press is sometimes abused; and that the potential for even more frequent abuse exists as the number of media channels continues to shrink and as control is more and more tightly gripped by fewer and fewer hands.

Thus the dilemma, a hardy two centuries old.

Press freedom must be preserved, or all else goes with it. Yet totally uncontrolled power is an uncomfortable presence in a free society. Is there any agency to which we would "dare commit" the mission of resolving the dilemma?

In the next chapters we'll wrestle with that one, probably with no more success than Franklin or Adams had.

10
Media Controls: Tried and Untried

Had this book examined almost any industry or institution other than the media in an effort to find out what makes it tick, we would very early have investigated the regulatory forces designed to establish standards and ensure quality of performance in that institution or industry.

For some institutions, such controls are in the form of government licensing, supplemented by internal policing (as in medicine and law). For most others, some government agency—national, state, or local—is charged with safeguarding the public interest insofar as standards and performance are concerned. Because the First Amendment has been an unyielding barrier to the establishment of any kind of government overview of the news media, we must look elsewhere to learn how standards are set and performance is monitored in the field of journalism.

A SPECIAL CASE

First, however, let us consider the case of the broadcast media, which do indeed operate under a kind of government licensing and appear much less well shielded by the First Amendment than is the case with print journalism.

Early in the broadcast era, when radio was the only such medium, the fledgling industry invited government into the picture as a sort of traffic cop. The limited spectrum of radio frequencies was hopelessly tangled; individual broadcasters poached on one another's broadcasting range at will. Anyone with a transmitter could set up in business on any frequency, whether or not it was already in use by someone else. So the broadcasters themselves called for a referee to sort out the claims to frequencies and allocate the limited number of spots on the broadcasting spectrum. No First Amendment implications were perceived by anyone, since the medium at that time was almost entirely enter- tainment- and advertising-oriented, with news a very minor appendage.

The supervisory role thus established is still carried out, now by the Fed- eral Communications Commission; its purview includes television as well as radio and in recent years its arm has been extended over cable systems also.

At first glance, the FCC's power over broadcasters seems to be broad and significant. Any radio or television broadcast station must be originally licensed by the FCC and then reviewed and relicensed every three years. The Commis- sion's equal time and fairness doctrines, discussed earlier, impinge directly on the freedom of the broadcast media to present the news.

In practice, however, the FCC's apparent power over the media has been eroding steadily. A persistent fight to bring radio and television under the wing of the First Amendment has been energetically waged by the networks (which are themselves insulated to some degree from FCC supervision, since only sta- tions are licensed, not networks as such).

At one time, for example, broadcasters were not permitted to editorialize, under FCC ruling; that prohibition was struck down by the courts.

The fairness doctrine was challenged in the case of an NBC-TV documentary on industrial pensions. The FCC called the program one-sided and demanded that NBC produce another program giving a balanced version. NBC refused, the issue went to court, and the FCC lost. The court's opinion included the significant observation that the broadcaster, not a government agency, has "both initial responsibility and primary responsibility" for editorial judgments.

The equal time doctrine also has been relaxed, to permit the presidential debates in 1960 and 1976. (Only two candidates debated; the numerous splinter nominees were not given "equal time.")

Another restrictive ruling, establishing the family viewing hour and for- bidding shows depicting violence or sex to be shown during early evening watching periods, was struck down by the courts in 1976. Again, most sig- nificantly, the ground for the decision was that the ruling violated the First Amendment. (The family viewing hour arrangement was not officially an FCC dictum; it was imposed by the National Association of Broadcasters and the networks. The court held, however, that FCC pressure was behind the NAB code change, and that the pressure had been unconstitutionally applied.)

Various attempts by other branches of government to interfere with the editorial decisions or operating methods of broadcasters have also been re- buffed, again with the First Amendment figuring prominently in the broad- casters' arguments.

CBS President Frank Stanton, in the "Selling of the Pentagon" case discussed in chapter 5, successfully resisted the attempt by a congressional committee to subpoena out-takes (film shot for a program but eventually not used) and reporters' notes, contending that this would be unconstitutional interference with press freedom.

TV reporter Daniel Schorr, in a case also discussed in chapter 5, made his refusal to reveal a confidential source to another congressional committee stick despite threats of contempt charges. He, too, stood on First Amendment rights.

Step by slow step, the broadcast media are beginning to succeed in a long effort to put themselves on the same footing as their print colleagues regarding First Amendment protections of free expression. The trend has resulted from several developments in the broadcast media and outside.

First, news has become an increasingly major factor in the broadcasting mix, not an incidental appendage. Today most Americans obtain most of their news and information from television. While entertainment and advertising still dominate, the broadcast media are clearly part of the news system of the nation. They thus are rightly entitled to First Amendment protection.

Second, by virtue of their emerging nature as major news media, the broadcasting industries have acquired a new dimension of power, hefty enough for them to use in asserting their rights.

Finally, the print media have at last come around to acknowledging their First Amendment kinship with broadcast news operations. For many years the newspapers were reluctant to make that acknowledgment; they viewed the broadcasters as entertainers and hucksters, not journalists. Some among the print media were not at all unhappy to see their chief competitors hamstrung by the FCC or under fire from Congress or other government agencies. But at least some print media spokespersons have had a considerable change of heart in recent years. As Eric Sevareid of CBS told a group of journalists in Washington in 1976:

> . . . until rather recently . . . those in the printed press who became disturbed by direct government assault on broadcasting were saying to us, "Look out, your end of the boat is sinking." That has greatly changed, thank heaven. We all know now that we occupy a common vessel. It is not compartmentalized.[3]

Broadcasters may not yet have a first-class seat on the boat. The FCC still exists and functions, though its clout has clearly been reduced where news broadcasting is concerned. It cannot yet be said that TV and radio journalists operate with as much freedom as do their print counterparts. But sooner or later, at least insofar as news and documentary programs are concerned, it seems inevitable that television and radio will come to share fully in the safeguards of the First Amendment. And then, as we must do now in the case of the print media, we shall have to look elsewhere than to government for the forces that set standards and ensure quality performance in these media.

WHAT ELSE IS THERE?

Although in virtually all instances the First Amendment has barred government attempts to control the actions of the news media (particularly the print media), critics of the media are not deterred from demanding that *something* be done, that *someone* establish principles to guide journalists and set up agencies to ensure that those principles are being respected.

Such critics—and also disinterested analysts of the press—propose that since the news media enjoy special constitutional protections, they must accept concomitant obligations. Since the media maintain their immunity from policing by conventional regulatory agencies, they must undertake to police themselves.

Journalists responded to such arguments by forming associations and drawing up codes of conduct or statements of principles. The earliest was the Canons of Journalism adopted by the then new American Society of Newspaper Editors in 1922. It was characterized by a good deal of admirable rhetoric and high-sounding principles, most of them generalizations.

Other journalistic organizations also wrote codes of ethics, among them the Newspaper Guild, the trade union organization for journalists; Sigma Delta Chi, the Society of Professional Journalists; the Associated Press Managing Editors Association; and the National Conference of Editorial Writers. In recent years, as public distrust of and dissatisfaction with the news media began to be evident, more and more groups have gotten into the code-writing act, including an organization of food writers and editors and another of sports writers. In 1975 the ASNE boiled down and revamped its 53-year-old canons, retitling the code "A Statement of Principles."

All of the codes, new and old, have a lofty ring, but they are not a meaningful response to the critics who asked the media to police themselves. For all of the codes—without exception—are toothless, without provision for enforcement.

This is not to say that codes are of no value. They do provide a general blueprint to right conduct for those journalists disposed to behave ethically in the first place. But they have virtually no influence on the occasional renegade who chooses deliberately to exploit the power of the press for unworthy ends; such a person has nothing to fear from the codes. They can't rescind a sinner's license to practice journalism, since there is no such license. They can't confiscate a press or close down a scandal sheet. As has been shown more than once, they can't even get the code violator tossed out of the organization that adopted the code. (Such a case came up in the early days of the ASNE, and the association couldn't bring itself to defrock its erring member, empty as even that gesture would have been as a policing action.)

Take a look at some excerpts from the ASNE's new Statement of Principles. [4] No one could fault the intent of the language. But as you read the quotes, compare the rhetoric with the realities, as we have explored them elsewhere in this book.

> The primary purpose of gathering and distributing news and opinion is to serve the general welfare by informing the people and enabling them to make judgments on the issues of the time. Newspapermen and women who abuse the power of their professional role for selfish motives or unworthy purposes are faithless to that public trust. [Certainly there's no arguing with that. But what can ASNE do about such faithless ones, except administer a verbal wrist slap?]

> Journalists must avoid impropriety and the appearance of impropriety as well as any conflict of interest or the appearance of conflict. They should neither accept anything nor pursue any activity that might compromise or seem to compromise their integrity. [Recall our discussion of "freebies" in chapter 6.]

> Significant errors of fact, as well as errors of omission, should be corrected promptly and permanently. [Again, think back to the discussion of the way corrections are typically handled by newspapers, taken up in chapter 9.]

I do not mean to hold the journalistic codes up to ridicule. They are indeed of value. But there is a danger in thinking that once a code has been drawn up and adopted, all the problems of unethical behavior have been dealt with, once and for all. Without enforcement machinery, codes are at best instruments of moral suasion. Yet truly effective enforcement machinery, directed from outside the industry, would run head-on into the First Amendment. Back to square one.

AROUND THE COUNCIL TABLE

In 1947 a blue-ribbon Commission on Freedom of the Press (often called the Hutchins Commission, since it was chaired by Robert Maynard Hutchins, Chancellor of the University of Chicago) reported on its extensive investigation into the present state and probable future of the press in America. Among the commission's recommendations was that an organization of national leaders be formed as an impartial council to monitor the performance of the news media. [5] This council would receive complaints from persons or groups who believed they had evidence of irresponsibility or abuse by the press, would investigate the charges, and then would issue a report either exonerating or reprimanding the publication involved. The publication would be expected to give space to the council's finding.

Such a national news council was needed, the Hutchins Commission asserted, because the press was not policing itself adequately. A monitor consisting of distinguished private citizens from many fields would be infinitely preferable to the establishment of a government overview agency, which the commission thought might otherwise be inevitable.

Most media managers, both print and broadcast, promptly and vehemently rejected the notion, seeing in it an unacceptable threat to press freedom. The report was filed on library shelves, to be assigned occasionally as required reading in journalism classes.

But the commission's idea persisted and eventually began to find expression. Five years after the Hutchins report, the British established a national press council, though on a basis somewhat different from that envisioned by the Hutchins proposal. It has functioned ever since, accepting complaints, investigating cases, and handing down judgments.

In the United States a few—a very few—editors experimented on their own with the press council idea on a local scale. Then in 1966 the Mellet Fund for a Free and Responsible Press asked educators in various parts of the country to join in an experiment with local press councils on a systematic basis. Councils were established and operated for a year or more in small towns in Illinois, California, and Oregon, and also in Seattle. Later a permanent media council was established for the city of Honolulu, and a statewide council was set up in Minnesota.

Finally, in 1973, the Twentieth Century Fund sponsored the establishment of a National News Council for the United States, charged primarily with keeping an eye on the "national news media"—the newsmagazines, the broadcast networks, the wire services, and a few major newspapers considered to be the only valid equivalents of Britain's national press.

What has been the contribution of the various efforts at voluntary citizen monitoring of press performance? Is this the answer to the dilemma voiced by Franklin and Adams? Has a safe agency finally been found to function as a quality control on the activities of the news media?

Well, not quite.

The press councils—local, state, and national—have had some salutary impact on the news media. There has been some consciousness-raising among media managers and owners. But the claims of success must be cautiously couched and narrowly qualified.[6]

Press councils, at any level, suffer from the same inherent weakness that has made the ethics codes relatively ineffectual. There is no meaningful way by which the council can enforce its judgments: a publisher or broadcaster who wants to cooperate with the council by publishing its findings on a particular case may do so; he may even abide by those findings, if he wishes. But the council has no means to force compliance with its rulings, or even to require the offending station or publication to acknowledge that a negative judgment has been rendered.

Local press councils were useful in Bend, Oregon, and Redwood City, California, because the publishers in those communities were hospitable to the idea. But those publishers presided over excellent publications, giving good service to the community. Publishers of papers that are short-changing their communities obviously will not set up a press council or heed its findings if someone else sets it up.

During the first two years of its existence, the National News Council dealt formally with 61 separate cases involving complaints about media performance. Of those, 54 resulted in a verdict upholding the medium involved or were dismissed for lack of substance. Only 5 complaints resulted in findings against the medium involved; two cases were still pending at the end of the two-year period.[7]

It is still too early to judge the National Council's effectiveness. (In their December 1976 newsletter the directors assert: "We're doing well, thank you: we have several important proposals on the burners. And media support has been most encouraging. . . .") But the record isn't particularly impressive, if one takes into account just the fact that the total number of complaints filed in two years was only 61. Considering the widespread incidence of consumer dissatisfaction with the performance of the media, the complaint total invites the conclusion that few among the public have much confidence that it would do any good to complain to the Council. And they may well be right.

The Council's own report on its first two years stresses that there is more awareness of the need for responsible performance among the media as a result of its efforts; perhaps so. But many of the cases mentioned in earlier chapters, involving unethical or irresponsible performance, date from this same two-year period, or even later.

The British council has been in operation for 24 years. It has dealt with many hundreds of complaints and cases. Yet some of the sleaziest, least responsible journalism in the world is published in Great Britain today. There are great and ethical British newspapers, too, of course. But they were both great and ethical long before the council came on the scene.

The basic problem with the press council approach remains that it is obliged to deal in moral pressure, and to depend upon the willingness of the media managers to be influenced by such pressure. The good guys respond, but they probably were making few missteps in any case; the bad guys thumb their noses at the council and its judgments. There is no way to *compel* respect for a council reprimand or finding, any more than there is to compel a journalist to respect the ASNE Statement of Principles. That is a limiting, even crippling weakness, if you are looking for an effective watchdog over media standards and performance. For a press council or for a code, true enforcement ability would inevitably mean recourse to the courts; that is, an agency of government would be getting into the act. And that would mean setting aside the First Amendment—something we as a nation could not permit to happen.

UNTRIED OPTIONS

Most of the other proposals advanced for quality controls on the news media would, one way or another, lead to some degree of government intervention in the functioning of the press. For that and other reasons, these other proposals have not, in most cases, been given much if any trial.

One such notion was originated by Jerome Barron, a professor of law, and has since been championed by him and a few others, mostly outside press circles.[8] Barron's thesis is that in this era of very few news channels, most of them under the control of great corporations or conglomerates, the public is effectively barred from access to the media. The few opportunities for feedback or rebuttal that individual consumers have are absolutely controlled by the media themselves.

If the First Amendment is to have real present meaning, Barron contends, it must be reinterpreted. Not only should it safeguard freedom to publish; it should also be reworded to safeguard the public's freedom of access. Barron would make it a constitutional right of individuals to obtain space in a newspaper or time on a broadcast outlet to respond to any attack by the news medium on an individual, an institution, or a cause.

Critics of the Barron proposal see two crucial flaws. For one thing, it implies that some referee—presumably the courts—would have to determine when an attack or mention in the press warranted the exercise of the right to respond. That would make the judiciary, in effect, co-editor or co-producer of the news. Such a revamping of the First Amendment could well lead to the end of press freedom in this nation.

A case that essentially embodied the Barron thesis has been heard by the Supreme Court. It involved a Florida politician who sought to force a Miami newspaper to give him space to respond to a criticism that had been published by the paper. He relied on a musty Florida statute long ago forgotten, but still on the books. The Supreme Court unanimously ruled against the politician in a decision that read, in part:

> The choice of material to go into a newspaper and the decisions made as to limitations on the size of the paper, and content, and treatment of public issues and public officials—whether fair or unfair—constitutes the exercise of editorial control and judgment. It has yet to be demonstrated how governmental regulations of this crucial process can be exercised consistent with First Amendment guarantees of a free press as they have evolved to this time.[9]

The meaning is plain: the Barron approach would conflict with the First Amendment free press safeguard as it has functioned for two centuries.

A second problem with the Barron proposal is a practical one. Should the Bill of Rights be rewritten to guarantee public access to the media, those media would be so flooded with complaints, rebuttals, and sur-rebuttals that the news media would literally be choked out of existence.

Still, the reasoning behind the proposal is appealing in this era of massive media and powerless consumers. As press critic Ben Bagdikian observes:

> . . . every paper should have a policy of right-of-reply for those who have been criticized in the paper or who have serious differences with the paper's editorial policy. I believe that statutory or court-ordered right-of-reply and access are fatal to press freedom, but I believe the practice of providing this kind of access to the news and editorial pages is an absolute necessity for an institution that is largely monopolistic.[10]

"Absolute necessity"—but not something to be dictated by an agency of government. Once more the dilemma.

VOICES FOR ALL

Another notion somewhat akin to Jerome Barron's proposal has been talked about by various persons, among them press critic Robert Cirino. This idea calls for radio and television broadcasters to provide specific time slots for the expression of views from all quarters of the political spectrum.

In other words, a certain amount of prime broadcast time would be set aside each day by all the networks and all local stations. That time would be divided among liberal, conservative, and various other groups on the national and local levels. The amount of time available to any one viewpoint would be determined by the size of the segment of the community that adhered to the viewpoint. Thus the Republican and Democratic time allocations would be established on the basis of the two parties' numerical showings in the last election. Other yardsticks would be used to make sure that even tiny ideological interest groups would get at least a few minutes to air their views. Proponents of this idea would expect the FCC or some similar agency to function as arbiter of the time allocations.

This idea has not yet been tried by commercial broadcasting (although the public broadcasting system and individual stations associated with it have been making time available to splinter groups of various kinds), partly because the networks and stations are understandably reluctant to surrender any of their most valuable broadcast time and partly because the extension of FCC power implied in the proposal would likely be resisted by all the media.

SUMMARY

In this chapter we have briefly inventoried various approaches to the imposition of quality controls on the news media.

We have noted the hazards of government supervision of the press, and the increasingly successful efforts of the broadcast media to wriggle out of the partial government control that has characterized their situation ever since they emerged on the media scene.

We have noted also the existence of codes of ethics and statements of principles—voluntary efforts by media groups to demonstrate their devotion to ethical, responsible performance. These are well-meaning, they have a modestly uplifting influence on already responsible media managers, and they are almost totally ineffectual where they are really needed: in improving the standards of the unscrupulous.

We have evaluated the limited success of press councils as watchdogs with some bark but no bite. We have also explored some of the fundamental flaws in as yet untried proposals for quality controls in the media, such as a constitutionally rooted right of consumers to have free access to the media to respond to attacks or to take issue with editorial positions.

The scene thus far has not yielded much evidence that standards and quality controls have a significant place among the factors that make the media tick. In the next chapter we'll identify some other, more hopeful, signs.

11
Are *Any* Controls at Work?

Chapter 10 suggested that some of the self-policing efforts of the news media are more show than substance; in the pinch, they have not proven impressively successful. It also pointed out that virtually all of the proposals for establishing *external* controls on press standards and performance sooner or later raise the specter of unconstitutional government restraint on the media, a specter we as a people cannot permit to emerge.

Yet chapter 10 ended on the assurance that there were signs that the seemingly hopeless dilemma could be at least partially resolved—in fact, was already partially resolved. What are those signs?

They are evident principally in the words and actions of some media leaders and of some rank-and-file workers in various journalistic enterprises.

In his report to the 1975 meeting of the American Society of Newspaper Editors, that group's president, Howard H. (Tim) Hays, concluded that

> our responsibilities as editors and our concomitant opportunities are greater than ever. We have never held more of the future in our hands. Whether the American public will continue to accept the irritations and disappointments inherent in a free press depends, now more than ever, on how wisely and responsibly we perform. [1 1]

The widely respected publisher of one of the nation's fine papers, the *Riverside* (California) *Press-Enterprise*, made two realistic and extremely important points in that brief conclusion to his report.

He acknowledged, as a fact of life about the media today, that their future freedom is not necessarily assured. Their functioning has antagonized many segments of the public, and it is conceivable that someday those segments could coalesce and wield enough leverage to change the protected status the press has so long enjoyed under the First Amendment.

Hays simultaneously acknowledged that such a disastrous outcome can be prevented only if the media themselves perform in a fashion that restores public confidence and willingness to accept the "irritations and disappointments" that almost inevitably are engendered by the operations of the media.

Hays is by no means alone among his journalistic colleagues in sensing the hazard confronting the media.

Norman E. Isaacs, former executive editor of the *Louisville Courier-Journal and Times,* former president and publisher of the *Wilmington* (Delaware) *News-Journal,* a chairman of the National News Council, and now on the faculty of the Columbia University Graduate School of Journalism, observes:

> Many American editors are deeply concerned over the extent of public antagonism to the press. The thoughtful among them know that the course that has been followed the past few decades has gone from low risk to high risk and now into open and serious danger. The mood of the public became frighteningly clear at the time former Vice-President Agnew put a torch to the smoldering brush fire of antagonism. Despite what has happened since to the fortunes of the Messrs. Nixon and Agnew and their henchmen, the bitterness about the press is still there.[12]

What, specifically, are concerned editors doing to ward off the possible consequences of growing public bitterness, to restore a feeling of trust in the media?

OMBUDSMEN—THE HARDY FEW

Some editors have established on their publications the position of ombudsman, an experienced staff member who functions as in-house critic of the newspaper's performance and expresses his opinions publicly, on the paper's editorial page or elsewhere in its columns.

The office of ombudsman is associated originally with Scandinavian governments. In those countries the ombudsman functions as the public's representative, empowered to accept citizen complaints about the heavy—or clumsy—hand of government and to investigate those complaints and right any wrongs that may have inspired them.

In the American media incarnation, the ombudsman does some of the same things for newspaper readers with a complaint or grievance. The ombudsman's office is a lightning rod for complaints directed at the paper's performance; the complaints are followed up and resolved, sometimes by public apology, sometimes by more concrete action suggested to management by the ombudsman. The frequent result: a reader who has been reassured that a humane concern exists within the mighty press engine, and who thereafter may not be heard so often among the critics. Moreover, since the correction process or apology has been public, the reassurance may rub off on many other readers as well.

Why do the ministrations of an ombudsman have any more influence on newspaper performance and public confidence than, say, the pronouncements of a press council? They are more effective for two reasons. It is a craft condition that members of the tightly knit staff on any media operation are keenly sensitive to their standing among their peers. A public spanking in the columns of their own publication can be a traumatic, lasting reminder not to make mistakes of fact or judgment that injure the rights of a reader.

Second, the ombudsman can respond promptly and decisively to a reader complaint; a press council is a diffuse, outside intermediary that takes far longer to deal with a charge from someone in the public and can't get much remedial action at best.

An effective ombudsman needs a sensitive and understanding ear (for reader complaints), a thick skin (to ward off the angry slings of his colleagues on the paper), and a meaningful writ of independence from the management of the operation. Without these characteristics, the ombudsman will likely fail in his or her tightrope-walking assignment.

Not all papers have been willing to try the experiment; most that have, as we noted of codes and press councils, are the better ones. Some have not found the device successful. But others, after a few false starts, have made it work surprisingly well. One of the pioneers, Ben Bagdikian, *Washington Post* ombudsman for a year, says that "the idea ought to continue because there seems no other way to provide systematic review of this major institution, and to do it in a way that is meaningful to the readers."[13]

Here are a few similarly positive evaluations from successful ombudsmen on other papers:

> The ombudsman symbolizes a purpose and is a constant reminder that there is an on-going effort at improvement. The effort becomes self-sustaining as people, especially those on a news staff, realize that the ombudsman not only exists but will continue to exist.—Bill Branstead, *St. Louis Post-Dispatch*

> Errors which call for correction, of course, get first attention. As to the public, every communication that comes my way gets answered by letter or phone. . . . [The reader] seems pleased, almost without exception thus far in my brief experience, with at least the concept that *The Star* cares enough about his opinions to have someone in there to whom he can go with his gripes and ideas. . . .—George Beveridge, *Washington Star*

> We begin with the charge that proper respect for the printed word established public accountability as a professional duty. It must become an article of faith, if you will, that when we err, we owe it to individuals and groups to set the record straight. And that is to be done with no defensive "yes, buts" either to mitigate the error or to spare the feelings of professional journalists. —J. Donald Brandt, *Wilmington* (Delaware) *News-Journal*

> [T]he press . . . is a necessary watchdog with certifiably sharp teeth. But who will watch the watchdog? Well, lacking a better solution, I think we are going to have to train him to watch himself. . . . We of the press don't wear our power gracefully. We are aloof, complacent, self-righteous, self-congratulatory, and sometimes downright arrogant. . . . I don't think we have to be loved—and I don't think there is any danger that we will be if we do our job properly. It is true that we as messengers must continue to deliver a lot of bad news.
>
> But I do think it would be good for us and the country if we were trusted more fully than we are—and hated and feared less.
>
> I think one way to win trust—if not affection—is to let in the light. To concede that the press is at least a quasi-public institution and accountable to the public. To accept a share of the spotlight we so effectively use on the rest of society.—Charles B. Seib, *Washington Post*.[14]

Charles Seib operates with perhaps more freedom than any other of the small company of ombudsmen around the nation's newspapers. He had not been on the *Post* staff before he took the position, and he has a five-year contract from Editor Ben Bradlee, so he can't be fired if the heat his columns generate gets too intense. Seib also has a franchise to range outside his own paper; he surveyed the performance of all the media in the 1976 presidential campaign and awarded an overall rating of C-minus.

Almost as much freedom is accorded to the ombudsman for the Louisville, Kentucky, papers owned by Barry Bingham, one of the most insistent advocates of responsible journalism among the ranks of leading editors and publishers.

The ombudsman device is too radical an approach for many newspapers. Seib notes:

> Newspapermen are notoriously sensitive to criticism, particularly to criticism in print. They can dish it out, but they are not very enthusiastic about accepting it.[15]

Painful as it may be, however, unsparing self-criticism has proven an invaluable physic for those papers sturdy enough to try it. As Bagdikian observes, "newspapers need it. They are profitable and stable, but they live in a world that is more precarious than most think."

Still, the ranks of the working ombudsmen in the country must be one of the most exclusive circles in the business. As that circle widens, so will the hope that the press can find sufficiently effective means of self-discipline to quiet the bitter, insistent voices demanding that something be done to place the massive power of the media under control.

OPEN LINES

Many editors who for one reason or another have chosen not to try the ombudsman approach have nonetheless taken note of the mood of the public and have tried to do something positive about it.

Some have attempted to expand significantly the lines of communication with readers. The *St. Petersburg* (Florida) *Times*, for example, has not only increased the space given to conventional letters to the editor, but has instituted a hotline service. Any reader who can't wait to write a letter can vent his or her protest or indignation by phone; a hotline recorder bank is constantly available for readers to use in dictating complaints. During certain hours each day an assistant to the editor waits by the phone to take calls and get prompt action on them. A regular hotline column runs in the paper, with excerpts from some of the calls received and a report of action taken or an explanation of what happened. Twice a month the paper also conducts a coupon poll of readers, soliciting opinions on issues in the news as well as on the paper's performance. The *Times* receives 25,000 to 30,000 reader communications of one form or another each year.

The *Chicago Tribune*, and many other papers both large and small, take a somewhat different approach to the improvement of reader relations. The *Tribune* carries a weekly column, "Reporting the News," devoted to explaining how and why the paper handled various news situations the previous week. This column, and others like it around the country (usually written by the managing editor or his assistant and often titled "Letter to the Reader" or something similar), in effect attempt to educate the readers on how the news is shaped, how the media tick. To achieve their objective, authors of such columns must be particularly careful not to patronize or talk down to readers.

Efforts to open more lines of communication with readers are no doubt useful. They are less dramatic and probably less successful than the ombudsman device, but they are steps in the right direction—toward restoring reader confidence in the integrity of the journalistic enterprise.

REVIEWS AND CRITICS

Professional critics of the media also play a part in establishing standards and monitoring performance. These critical voices are hybrids, neither insiders nor outsiders but a little of both. They are persons who are now in the journalism field, or have been in the past; thus their evaluations and appraisals are founded on an intimate knowledge of the workings of the media. But their commentaries are disseminated not by the medium under review (as is the case with the ombudsman's critique), but in specialized journals or books, or occasionally in competing media of general circulation.

Such individual critics as A. J. Liebling, Ben Bagdikian, and Edward Jay Epstein have published searching and sometimes scathing assessments of the media of their eras. Their books have not been best-sellers, however, and their impact has been felt more within some circles of the media (some, not all) than by the consuming public. Moreover, even within the media their efforts have often been discounted by editors or producers who scorn them as professional carpers, fouling their own nests.[16]

It has been more difficult for the media managers to summarily dismiss the efforts of the continuing reviews of press performance represented by such publications as *Nieman Reports*, put out for the last three decades by the Nieman Foundation of Harvard University; *Columbia Journalism Review*, produced by Columbia University; or *The Quill*, monthly publication of the 30,000-member Society of Professional Journalists, Sigma Delta Chi. All three publications have dealt in hard-hitting, authoritative evaluations of specific cases of media malpractice. They do not reach large consumer audiences, to be sure, but what they have to say is read with care in the editorial offices, newsrooms, and studios around the country. These publications, particularly *Columbia Journalism Review*, undoubtedly have had more to do with setting and enforcing ethical standards in journalism than all the codes ever written.

The monitoring efforts of the established journals have been supplemented sporadically by local reviews, many of them short-lived and most of them strident in tone.

The first of these was the *Chicago Journalism Review*, founded in 1968 by staff members of the Chicago media who were disgusted by the nature of the coverage given to the Democratic National Convention and associated events. Its contents included accounts written (sometimes anonymously) by still-active writers for the Chicago newspapers and broadcast outlets, presenting the "inside scoop" on stories mishandled, intrastaff squabbles, and management lapses. Imitators cropped up in Denver, Providence, New York, Portland, and elsewhere. Most had very limited circulations, however, and tended toward preoccupation with in-house feuds and office gossip. An exception is New York–based *(MORE)*, which is both hard-hitting and nationally circulated; but most of the reviews did not stay on the scene long enough to be truly effective upholders of standards or monitors of performance.

The professional critics and the press reviews have tried to do the job of quality control, and to some extent they have succeeded. But most persons, including those directly involved with the media, would probably find it difficult to take issue with this observation from the 1974 *Tornillo* opinion of the Supreme Court.

[T]he monopoly of the means of communication allows for little or no critical analysis of the media except in professional journals of very limited readership.

IDEAS AND INDIVIDUALS

This brings us, finally, to the point to which any writer about the functioning of the news media must eventually come: our best hope for responsible journalism, sensitive to ethical standards and willing to accept its public service obligations, lies in the stubborn persistence of an idea and in the consciences of the women and men who staff the news media. The persisting idea is the simple, central ethic of journalism—to inform the public as honestly, as fairly, and as completely as possible about the world. The attraction of that idea was cited earlier in this book as one of the factors that draw persons to work in the news media. And—so far as my experience runs—it is an idea that still lives meaningfully in the minds of a great many journalists. It is the most powerful, most pervasive quality control that exists within the news media.

Admittedly, not all the journalists who believe in this central ethic and want to respond to it are able to do so. They are limited by the organizational context in which they must work.

In an episode that occurred in 1977 there was a graphic reminder of that fact of life, but also a ray of hope for those who believe that the individual integrity of journalists can be an effective force for improving the press. The case involved the Panax group of newspapers, 40 small dailies and weeklies located mostly in the Midwest. The owner of the group had sent to all of his editors two "explosive" articles aimed at President Jimmy Carter, requesting that they be run as front page news. Most of the Panax editors complied with the request, but two editors of Michigan dailies in the group balked. David Rood of the *Escanaba Daily Press* and Robert Skuggen of the *Marquette Mining Journal* protested to the chain management that the stories were really editorials, laced with irresponsible and unsubstantiated "innuendo and insinuations." They offered to put the pieces on the opinion page, but refused the request to run them on page one as straight news. To comply, they maintained, would be a breach of journalistic standards and a disservice to their readers.

The chain owner held to his position, and so did the two editors. One resigned rather than run the "news" articles, and the other was fired after he refused to resign.

To that point the affair had followed a depressingly familiar pattern. Such confrontations between idealistic staff members and less principled superiors have taken place before, and with similar outcomes. But this time there were some unusual developments.

The editors' stand for journalistic ethics caught the attention of their two communities. Citizen groups were organized, town meetings were held; there was talk of boycott, and a formal protest was filed with the National News Council. Several other staff members of the two papers resigned in sympathy with Rood and Skuggen.

The members of the National News Council reviewed the case and voted to censure the chain owner for "a gross disservice to accepted American journalistic standards." Leading professional journals such as *The Quill* and *Columbia Journalism Review* strongly supported the editors and decried the tactics of the chain management.

Soon the chain announced the hiring of an editorial director, a post new in the organization. The author of the two hatchet job articles was dismissed as head of the chain's New York bureau. The two editors were not reinstated (both said they wouldn't return to Panax); but they promptly found new jobs on other papers. And the citizen groups laid plans for continuing watchdog efforts in the two communities.[17]

Admittedly, the Panax affair doesn't represent a total and shining triumph of individual integrity over unethical ownership; it was a modest, partial victory at best. But the way the episode unfolded suggests that staff members who have reason to object to lax standards further up the organizational line have more than a choice between suffering in silence or becoming jobless martyrs. It suggests that several forces working in concert—principled reporters and editors, an alerted and organized community agency, and national monitors to give an amplified voice to both—can bring to bear a pressure on backsliding management that none of these elements alone could generate.

Does the Panax case represent a hopeful straw in the wind? Has a precedent for combined action been set that will give the National News Council enhanced leverage as well as provide a channel through which the ethical convictions of rank-and-file journalists can find effective expression? Or was it an isolated, aberrant instance, unlikely to be repeated? By the time you read this the answers to those questions will possibly be clearer than they are at this moment of writing.

Perhaps one clarifying observation should be entered here. My reference above to the importance of the role of individual integrity, followed by the Panax anecdote, may have left the impression that I see the media as staffed by two types: unscrupulous, unprincipled owners and publishers on the one hand, and clear-eyed, ethical junior staff members on the other. That is not the case at all. There are responsible, ethical owners as well as responsible, ethical reporters and editors; it would be absurd to contend that any particular position on the ladder of authority, any particular job category in the media hierarchy, is a unique repository of journalistic virtue and respect for standards. There are ethical journalists at every staff level, from publisher's office to city hall beat; and the unscrupulous practitioners are equally widely distributed. As a practical matter, however, as the Panax case illustrates, it is the degree of responsibility that obtains at the ownership level that often is the most critical and overriding.

Norman Isaacs, in the Washington and Lee speech quoted from earlier in this chapter, offered a pessimistic assessment of the prevalence of respect for the concept of quality journalism among media owners, who make many of the final decisions that determine how good a news operation can be:

> [T]here are perhaps no more than 20 to 30 newspapers in the land with a demonstrated record of continuous public service and which allocate their resources in such a way as to provide what can be termed distinguished journalism, if not all of the time at least much of the time. But 20 out of a total of 1,750 daily papers is .0114 percent [he meant 1.14 percent] of the list. Of these 1,750 papers about 70 percent are now owned by corporate chains. . . .[18]

I would not put the percentage of consistently good papers as low as does Isaacs. But I would agree with two implications of his comment: (1) that idealism in the ranks can often be frustrated by a more callous conscience in the office of the publisher or the network producer; and (2) that such frustration takes place more often in chain and group operations, both print and broadcast, than in independently owned publications or stations.

From these points, it seems to me, a fundamental premise derives: the journalistic ethic is alive and well among many of the men and women in the news business today, but often it cannot find effective expression because of organizational constraints, particularly within corporate groups and chains.

I have no research findings or statistical tables to support that premise, only a lifetime of experience in, and observation of, the news media. But if you are willing to accept the premise on that admittedly tenuous basis, then perhaps you will also buy my contention that something *can* and *should* be done to improve the odds for those media persons who would give us quality journalism if they could.

TWO MODEST PROPOSALS

It would be neither difficult nor unfair, for example, to amend the tax laws that, as they are now drawn, actually *promote* the expansion of chains and groups. For the media and other enterprises as well, the laws provide that profits that are plowed into the acquisition of additional operating capacity of a business (for a newspaper chain, that means adding new papers to the group) can largely escape taxation. Ordinarily a dollar of profit earned by a corporation would shrink to roughly 30 cents after being subjected first to the corporate tax and then to additional taxation when it is passed on as dividend income to stockholders. But if that dollar is spent to acquire new operating capacity for the business (another paper for the chain), it is not taxed *at all.* Thus a chain management can bid for a new acquisition with what are, in effect, 30-cent dollars. The chain can therefore afford to pay more than three times the value of a newspaper property as measured by conventional standards.

Individual owners understandably find it hard to turn down the astronomically inflated offers the chains wave under their noses. So year by year the groups grow larger—and fewer. Now it has come to the point that the largest groups are beginning to swallow up already established smaller groups, as well as the few remaining individually owned papers. In 1976 the Newhouse group successfully bid more than $300,000,000 (a record price for a newspaper property) to acquire the Booth chain of small Michigan papers plus *Parade* magazine.

It would be simple for the Congress to change the tax laws so that they would not continue to foster the growth of chain journalism. I submit that it should be done.

I also believe that it would be possible—without raising any significant First Amendment hazards—to employ the antitrust laws to limit the number of newspapers any single owner or corporation may control. Bagdikian points out that "one such corporation owns 50 American daily newspapers in 17 states. Should anyone have such power over the basic information given to so many people every day?"[19]

Let me repeat so that the record will be clear: not all chain or group papers are giving poor journalistic service; some are among the best in the country. And there are plenty of shoddy independent papers. But the blunt fact remains: the force of the journalistic ethic that motivates so many men and women in journalism has a better chance of expression in media run by local owners than in those that are almost inevitably affected by the corporate philosophy prevalent in groups and chains.

With ownership more widely distributed, the power of the central ethic of journalism would have more breathing room and a better chance to hold its own. And we consumers would have a better chance at the quality of journalism we have a right to expect from an institution given special constitutional status in our system.

In the broadcast media there already exist FCC limitations on the number of radio and television stations a given owner may control. However, because the overall number of channels available is limited—particularly in television—the fifty largest television chains or groups have three-quarters of the total television audience. And the networks have become parts of conglomerates with varied corporate interests, some of them potentially in conflict with the journalistic obligations of the networks.

No simple measures suggest themselves as ways to improve upon this broadcast picture. But the inevitable spread of cable may bring about a diversity of voices and a counter to the concentration in the broadcast field. The necessity then will be to ensure that the cable systems do not fall into the monopoly or conglomerate pattern, and that sufficient channels are reserved for public access and the protection of the public interest. These ends can be achieved by limiting group ownership of cable systems, and by exercising care in drawing up local cable franchises.

Both the media and the nation will be healthier if the most powerful existing internal control on the quality of media performance—the devotion of the majority of journalists to the central ethic of the profession—is given maximum opportunity to be dominant among the factors that make the media tick.

SUMMARY

In this final chapter we have turned from proposals for external quality controls on the news media to examine the nature and effectiveness of controls instituted by, or inherent in, the media themselves.

The ombudsman, an idea borrowed from Scandinavian experiments with a "people's protector" in government, is among these. There are few ombudsmen on American newspapers as yet (and none in broadcasting), but where they have been given a chance to do their job they have significantly improved relationships with readers and helped to restore public confidence in the news media.

We noted, too, efforts by many papers to open lines of communication with the public, in an attempt to reduce the antagonism toward and lack of understanding of the press evident in many sectors of society. Hotlines and "Letter from the Editor" columns have some educational effect, but have achieved less restoration of confidence than have the ombudsmen.

Professional journalistic critics, both individuals and specialized publications, have functioned to some degree as quality controls. But they have been perceived more as outsiders than as insiders by the media, and there has been no means of ensuring that their counsels and admonitions would be heeded.

Finally, we looked into the last, best hope we consumers have that journalistic standards and performance will meet the needs of our democratic system: the simple yet powerful appeal of the central ethic of journalism and the surprisingly large number of women and men in the field who try to adhere to that ethic, despite organizational constraints.

The journalists dedicated to reporting the news fairly and fully need some help from us to reduce structural pressures that inhibit them in that mission. We can give them that help without in any sense abandoning vital First Amendment protections, first by changing tax laws that have the effect of encouraging the growth of chains, and second by setting limits on the number of media enterprises a single ownership can control.

CONCLUSION

The purpose of this book has been to give you some understanding of the internal and external forces and influences that cause the news media to function as they do.

We have not made a minute, definitive dissection of the media. Much, much more could be said about what makes the media tick. But many of the most pertinent points have been touched upon, and the bibliography that follows lists many sources from which you may gain other insights and viewpoints. I very much hope that any reader who has come this far will make use of that bibliography and draw upon the information and the interpretations to which it will lead.

The subject of this book, and of the series of which it is part, is of urgent importance to any citizen in present-day society. As important as economics. As important as history. As important as political science.

In an effort to emphasize that we perceive reality only through intermediaries, Plato described a small group of cave dwellers who gained their impressions of the outside world by watching the flickering shadows on the cave walls as persons or animals passed before the fire outside the mouth of the cave.

The technology has changed, but not the relationship. Since we still must depend, like the cave people, on the shadows of reality cast by the news media, it follows that we need to learn as much as we can about how those shadows are fashioned, how much they are distorted, and how faithful to reality they may be.

Our survival as a free society—indeed, the survival of the world itself—directly depends upon how clearly we and others perceive those pictures of reality, and how well we understand the capabilities and the limitations of the media machines that project the pictures for us.

Notes

SECTION ONE

1. Robert H. Estabrook, "Country Editor: Dream, Nightmare?" *The Masthead*, 28, no. 2 (Summer 1976), 13.
2. James R. Reston, "Notes on the Press," *Nieman Reports*, 29, no. 1 (Spring 1975), 11–14.
3. For details on the Chicago case see Michael Hirsh, "The Sins of Sears Are Not News in Chicago," *Columbia Journalism Review*, 15, no. 2 (July/Aug. 1976), 29–30.
4. Reston, "Notes on the Press," p. 12.
5. "A Press Release and a News Story," *Columbia Journalism Review*, editor's comment section, 14, no. 4 (Nov./Dec. 1975), 6.
6. Jeff Greenfield, "Down to the Last Detail," *Columbia Journalism Review*, 14, no. 6 (Mar./April 1976), 17.
7. Marvin Barrett, ed., *Moments of Truth? The Fifth Alfred I. DuPont–Columbia University Survey of Broadcast Journalism* (New York: Thomas Y. Crowell, 1975), p. 176.
8. Ibid., p. 156.
9. Most of the correspondence between W. B. Jones of Xerox and Mr. White is to be found in "What E. B. White Told Xerox," *Columbia Journalism Review*, 15, no. 3 (Sept./Oct. 1976), 52–54. The entire exchange was distributed by Xerox to interested persons in the press and education.

10. "The New Ballyhoo!!!" *Columbia Journalism Review,* 15, no. 3 (Sept./Oct. 1976), 39–44.

11. Sewell's views are expressed in detail in an interview by Robert Farquhar, "Sewell: Forget Gimmickry, Give Readers the News," *Associated Press Managing Editors News,* no. 83 (May 1975), 1, 5–6.

12. Edwin Diamond, "Would You Welcome, Please, Henry and Liv and Jackie and Erica!" *Columbia Journalism Review,* 14, no. 3 (Sept./Oct. 1975), 42–46.

13. Details of the *Banner* survey were reported in a *New York Times* News Service story released for publication on 26 Sept. 1976, in all papers subscribing to the service.

14. Quoted in Barrett, ed., *Moments of Truth?* pp. 98–99.

15. Quoted in Philip Revzin, "The Television Era: Entertainment, Action Are Major Ingredients of the Local TV News," *The Wall Street Journal,* 15 Oct. 1976, 1, 23. (The quote appears on p. 23.)

16. Quoted in "Remark: All Those Pretty, TV News Anchormen," *The Quill,* 63, no. 9 (Oct. 1975), 9.

17. "The New Look of TV News," *Newsweek,* 88, no. 15 (11 Oct. 1976), 68–81. The Sanders quote appears on p. 81.

18. Marvin Barrett, "Broadcast Journalism Since Watergate," *Columbia Journalism Review,* 14, no. 6 (Mar./April 1976), 73–83.

19. "The New Look of TV News," p. 77.

20. Quoted in *Journalism Newsletter* (College of Journalism, University of Maryland), 24 (1975), 1.

SECTION TWO

1. Schorr made the comments during an interview on the CBS "Sixty Minutes" program broadcast on 26 Sept. 1976.

2. John P. Robinson, "The Press as King Maker: What Surveys from Last Five Campaigns Show," *Journalism Quarterly,* 51, no. 4 (Winter 1974), 587–94, 606.

3. From a speech delivered on 21 Nov. 1975 at a symposium at the University of Oregon. The text of the speech was later published in a booklet, *The Responsibilities of Power* (Eugene: University of Oregon School of Journalism, 1976); the quoted observation appears on p. 13.

4. Timothy Crouse, *The Boys on the Bus* (New York: Ballantine Books, 1972), p. 39. Reprinted by permission of Random House, Inc.

5. Ibid., p. 48.

6. Morris Janowitz, "Professional Models in Journalism: The Gatekeeper and the Advocate," *Journalism Quarterly,* 52, no. 4 (Winter 1975), 618–26, 662.

7. Ibid., p. 626.

8. In a speech delivered on 8 Oct. 1976 at American University, and reported in an Associated Press news story published on 9 Oct. 1976.

9. Quoted in Laurence Stern, "The Daniel Schorr Affair," *Columbia Journalism Review,* 15, no. 1 (May/June 1976), 20–26. Quote appears on p. 21.

10. John W. C. Johnstone, "Organizational Constraints on Newswork," *Journalism Quarterly*, 53, no. 1 (Spring 1976), 5–13.
11. Ibid., p. 5.
12. Quoted in Benno C. Schmidt, Jr., and Harold Edgar, "S-1—Would the new bill amount to an official secrets law—and could it work?" *Columbia Journalism Review*, 14, no. 6 (March/April 1976), 18–21. Quote appears on p. 18.
13. See "A Bow to Big Brother?" *Newsweek*, 88, no. 10 (6 Sept. 1976), 69–70.
14. Quoted in John L. Hulteng, *The Messenger's Motives* (Englewood Cliffs, N.J.: Prentice-Hall, 1976), p. 222.
15. Ibid., p. 224.
16. Ibid., p. 225.
17. Edward Jay Epstein, "The Grand Cover Up," *The Wall Street Journal*, 19 April 1976, p. 10.
18. Hugh M. Culbertson, *Veiled News Sources—Who and What Are They?* ANPA News Research Bulletin No. 3 (14 May 1975), 9.
19. Quoted in "Gossip Mania," *Newsweek*, 87, no. 21 (24 May 1976), 56–64. Quote appears on p. 56.
20. Quoted in "Forewarning," a book review by Stephen Hess, *Columbia Journalism Review*, 14, no. 2 (July/Aug. 1975), 56–57.
21. "Fulbright on the Press," *Columbia Journalism Review*, 14, no. 4 (Nov./Dec. 1975), 39–45.
22. *News Media Facilities in the State Legislatures,* a report by the Legislative Research Office of the state of Oregon, 75: 128 (23 June 1976).
23. Hulteng, *The Messenger's Motives,* p. 43.
24. "The 'Contagion' Issue," *Newsweek*, 86, no. 14 (6 Oct. 1975), 77–78.
25. Ibid., p. 77.
26. Neil Hickey, "Terrorism and Television." Excerpted with permission from the 31 July 1976 issue of *TV Guide*® Magazine. Copyright © 1976 by Triangle Publications, Inc., Radnor, Pennsylvania.
27. Ibid.
28. Ibid.
29. Neil Hickey, "The Medium in the Middle." Excerpted with permission from the 7 August 1976 issue of *TV Guide*® Magazine. Copyright © 1976 by Triangle Publications, Inc., Radnor, Pennsylvania.
30. Ibid.
31. Ibid.
32. Vermont Royster, "More Competence Is What News Media Need Most." Excerpted with permission from the 17 April 1976 issue of *TV Guide*® Magazine. Copyright © 1976 by Triangle Publications, Inc., Radnor, Pennsylvania.
33. Edith Efron, "Is There a Network News Bias?" Excerpted with permission from *TV Guide*® Magazine. Copyright © 1970 by Triangle Publications, Inc. Radnor, Pennsylvania. The article was republished in the June 1970 issue of *Seminar Quarterly,* and in Michael C. Emery and Ted Curtis Smythe, *Readings in Mass Communication: Concepts and Issues in the Mass Media* (Dubuque, Iowa: Wm. C. Brown, 1974), pp. 456–61.
34. For additional details see "Expose Thy Neighbor," *Newsweek*, 88, no. 26 (27

Dec. 1976), 55; and "California Split: Dog Bites Dog," *Time,* 108, no. 26 (27 Dec. 1976), 26.

35. Dan G. Drew, "Reporters' Attitudes, Expected Meetings with Source, and Journalistic Objectivity," *Journalism Quarterly,* 52, no. 2 (Summer 1975), 219–24, 271.

SECTION THREE

1. Charles Kuralt, "Journalism is crisis-ridden; the country is not," *American Society of Newspaper Editors Bulletin,* no. 592 (January 1976), 13–15.

2. Linda A. Dangerfield, Hunter P. McCartney, and Ann T. Starcher, "How Did Mass Communication, as Sentry, Perform in the Gasoline 'Crunch'?" *Journalism Quarterly,* 52, no. 2 (Summer 1975), 316–20.

3. Quoted in Marvin Barrett, "Broadcast Journalism since Watergate," *Columbia Journalism Review,* 14, no. 6 (March/April 1976), 73–83. The quote, from an unidentified station staff member, appears on p. 81.

4. "The New Look of TV News," *Newsweek,* 88, no. 15 (11 Oct. 1976), 68–81.

5. Quoted in "The New Ballyhoo!!!" *Columbia Journalism Review,* 15, no. 3 (Sept./Oct. 1976), 39–44.

6. David K. McMillan, "Wolf! . . . once too often . . . ," *American Society of Newspaper Editors Bulletin,* no. 592 (Jan. 1976), 8–9.

7. Kuralt, "Journalism is crisis-ridden."

8. Frank K. Kelly, "Ethics of Journalism in a Century of Change," *Nieman Reports,* 22, no. 2 (June 1968), 12–15.

9. Speech delivered at the University of Texas School of Communication, 9 March 1974.

10. Agnew's first speech attacking the television networks was delivered at Des Moines, Iowa, on 13 Nov. 1969. The text is reprinted in Michael C. Emery and Ted Curtis Smythe, *Readings in Mass Communication: Concepts and Issues in the Mass Media,* 2nd ed. (Dubuque, Iowa: Wm. C. Brown, 1974), pp. 497–506.

11. Edith Efron, "Is There a Network News Bias?" Reprinted from *TV Guide,* copyright © 1970, Triangle Publications, Inc. The article was also reprinted in the June 1970 issue of *Seminar Quarterly.*

12. Ibid.

13. Quoted in Charles E. Hayes, "You Missed One of the Best Programs in Recent Years," *American Society of Newspaper Editors Bulletin,* no. 587 (May/June 1975), 3–5.

14. Vermont Royster, "More Competence Is What News Media Need Most." Reprinted from the April 1976 issue of *TV Guide* magazine. Copyright © 1976 by Triangle Publications, Inc.

15. Edwin Diamond, "The New Campaign Journalism," *Columbia Journalism Review,* 14, no. 6 (March/April 1976), 11–14.

16. Ibid., p. 14.

17. From an editorial in the *Eugene* (Oregon) *Register-Guard,* 5 Oct. 1976.

18. From a speech delivered on 8 March 1975 at the University of Texas School of Communication.

19. "Publish and Perish," *Newsweek,* 87, no. 11 (15 March 1976), 66, 69.
20. Ibid., p. 69.
21. Dan Carmichael, "Hawaii Saying Aloha to Heidi," *Columbia Journalism Review,* 14, no. 2 (July/Aug. 1975), 18–19.

SECTION FOUR

1. Quoted in *Journalism Quarterly,* 52, no. 2 (Summer 1975), 325.
2. Quoted in a speech by Norman E. Isaacs at Washington and Lee University, Lexington, Va. The text was published together with others in booklet form by Washington and Lee in 1975, under the title *Social Responsibilities: Journalism, Law, Medicine.*
3. From a speech delivered at the Washington Journalism Center, 3 June 1976.
4. The full text of the new ASNE Statement of Principles was published in *The American Society of Newspaper Editors Bulletin,* no. 591 (Nov./Dec. 1975), 22.
5. Commission on Freedom of the Press, *A Free and Responsible Press* (Chicago: University of Chicago Press, 1947).
6. For a detailed account of the local press council experiments, see William L. Rivers et al., *Back-Talk: Press Councils in America* (San Francisco: Canfield Press, 1972).
7. The National News Council, *In the Public Interest* (New York: The National News Council, 1975).
8. For a complete exposition of the Barron proposal, see Jerome A. Barron, *Freedom of the Press for Whom? The Rise of Access to the Mass Media* (Bloomington: University of Indiana Press, 1973).
9. *Miami Herald* v. *Tornillo* (418 U.S. 241), June 1974.
10. Ben H. Bagdikian, "Press Profits from Self-Criticism," *The Masthead,* 28, no. 1 (Spring 1976), 3–5.
11. Howard H. Hays, "President Hays' Message," *American Society of Newspaper Editors Bulletin,* no. 587 (May/June 1975), 16–17.
12. Isaacs, "Journalism's Ethics—1975–2000," a speech delivered at Washington and Lee University and published in 1975 in *Social Responsibilities.*
13. Bagdikian, "Press Profits from Self-Criticism."
14. All four quotations came from a symposium, "The Role of the Ombudsman/ Media Critic," *The Masthead,* 28, no. 1 (Spring 1976), 3–15.
15. Ibid., p. 14.
16. Some of the best works include Ben H. Bagdikian, *The Information Machines, Their Impact on Men and the Media* (New York: Harper & Row, 1971), and *The Effete Conspiracy and Other Crimes by the Press* (New York: Harper & Row, 1972); Edward Jay Epstein, *News from Nowhere: Television and the News* (New York: Random House, 1973), and *Between Fact and Fiction: The Problem of Journalism* (New York: Vintage Books, 1975); A. J. Liebling, *The Press* (New York: Ballantine, 1964).
17. See Roger Boye, "The Panax Dispute Remains a Hot Issue," *The Quill,* 65, no. 8 (September 1977), 10–11; "What Passes for News at Panax," Editor's com-

ment, *Columbia Journalism Review,* 16, no. 3 (Sept./Oct. 1977), 6–7; and John L. Hulteng, "The Crux of Panax: The Performance or the Power?" *The Quill,* 65, no. 9 (October 1977), 23–25, 29.

18. Issacs, "Journalism's Ethics."
19. From a speech, "Journalism Ethics in the Post-Watergate World," delivered at Washington and Lee University and later published in *Social Responsibilities.*

Additional Reading

BOOKS

BAGDIKIAN, BEN H., *The Information Machines, Their Impact on Men and the Media.* New York: Harper & Row, 1971.
   What computerization, cable television, and other technological advances may mean for the media of the present and the future.

BARRETT, MARVIN, ed., *Moments of Truth? The Fifth Alfred I. DuPont–Columbia University Survey of Broadcast Journalism.* New York: Thomas Y. Crowell, 1975.
   Critique of broadcasting during the 1973–75 period, with cases, comments on trends, and citations of outstanding performance.

BARRON, JEROME A., *Freedom of the Press for Whom? The Rise of Access to the Mass Media.* Bloomington: Indiana University Press, 1973.
   A full exposition of Barron's reinterpretation of the First Amendment to embrace public access as well as freedom to publish.

BERNSTEIN, CARL, AND BOB WOODWARD, *All the President's Men.* New York: Simon & Schuster, 1974.

COMMISSION ON FREEDOM OF THE PRESS, *A Free and Responsible Press.* Chicago: University of Chicago Press, 1947.
   Report of a blue ribbon commission appointed to appraise the press and its future. Not recent, admittedly, but important because many current developments in the press stem from viewpoints advanced in this report.

CROUSE, TIMOTHY, *The Boys on the Bus.* New York: Ballantine, 1972.
   A penetrating and readable analysis of how the traveling press corps covered one sequence of presidential primary campaigns.

DENNIS, EVERETTE E., AND WILLIAM L. RIVERS, *Other Voices: The New Journalism in America*. San Francisco: Canfield Press, 1974.

DIAMOND, EDWIN, *The Tin Kazoo: Television, Politics, and the News*. Cambridge: MIT Press, 1975.

EMERY, MICHAEL C., AND TED CURTIS SMYTHE, eds., *Readings in Mass Communication: Concepts and Issues in the Mass Media,* 2nd and 3rd eds. Dubuque, Iowa: Wm. C. Brown, 1974, 1977.
Both editions of this book contain helpful articles on mass media problems.

EPSTEIN, EDWARD JAY, *Between Fact and Fiction: The Problem of Journalism*. New York: Vintage Books, 1975.
Comments from a contemporary press critic.

————, *News from Nowhere: Television and the News*. New York: Random House, 1973.

GLESSING, ROBERT, *The Underground Press in America*. Bloomington: Indiana University Press, 1970.

HOHENBERG, JOHN, *Free Press, Free People: The Best Cause*. New York: Free Press, 1973.
The arguments for an independent press, eloquently made by a veteran journalist and educator on the basis of domestic and international cases.

HULTENG, JOHN L., *The Messenger's Motives*. Englewood Cliffs, N.J.: Prentice-Hall, 1976.
A discussion of ethical problems facing persons who work in the media of mass communication.

KRIEGHBAUM, HILLIER, *Pressures on the Press*. New York: Thomas Y. Crowell, 1972.
An inventory of the tugs and hauls on the media.

LEROY, DAVID J., AND CHRISTOPHER H. STERLING, eds., *Mass News: Practices, Controversies, and Alternatives*. Englewood Cliffs, N.J.: Prentice-Hall, 1973.
A balanced collection of essays and appraisals.

MERRILL, JOHN C., *Existential Journalism*. New York: Hastings House, 1977.
Detailed philosophical probing into one of the motivations to which some journalists respond.

MEYER, PHILIP, *Precision Journalism: A Reporter's Introduction to Social Science Methods*. Bloomington: Indiana University Press, 1973.

PEMBER, DON R., *Mass Media in America,* 2nd ed. Palo Alto, Ca.: Science Research Associates, 1977.
A comprehensive introductory text covering all the media.

————, *Mass Media Law*. Dubuque, Iowa: Wm. C. Brown, 1977.
Sound introduction to various aspects of law affecting the media. Clear, nontechnical.

PORTER, WILLIAM E., *Assault on the Media*. Ann Arbor: University of Michigan Press, 1976.
How the Nixon administration tried to intimidate the media.

RIVERS, WILLIAM L., ET AL., *Back-Talk: Press Councils in America*. San Francisco: Canfield Press, 1972.

RUBIN, BERNARD, *Media, Politics and Democracy.* New York: Oxford University Press, 1977.

SANDMAN, PETER M., DAVID M. RUBIN, AND DAVID B. SACHSMAN, *Media: An Introductory Analysis of American Mass Communication,* 2nd ed. Englewood Cliffs, N.J.: Prentice-Hall, 1977.
A critical but fair appraisal.

SCHRAMM, WILBUR, *Men, Messages and Media.* New York: Harper & Row, 1973.
A concise, graceful introductory text.

WOLFE, TOM, *The New Journalism.* New York: Harper & Row, 1973.

ARTICLES

BARRETT, MARVIN, "Broadcast Journalism since Watergate," *Columbia Journalism Review,* 14, no. 6 (1976), 73–83.
An update of the DuPont–Columbia University survey.

"California Split: Dog Bites Dog," *Time,* 108, no. 26 (1976), 26.
One newspaper criticizes the performance of another.

CARMICHAEL, DAN, "Hawaii Saying Aloha to Heidi," *Columbia Journalism Review,* 14, no. 2 (1975), 18–19.
A case in journalistic ethics.

"The 'Contagion' Issue," *Newsweek,* 86, no. 14 (1975), 77–78.
Does publishing news about assassination attempts inspire imitators to action?

DANGERFIELD, LINDA A., HUNTER P. MCCARTNEY, AND ANN T. STARCHER, "How Did Mass Communication, as Sentry, Perform in the Gasoline 'Crunch'?" *Journalism Quarterly,* 52, no. 2 (1975), 316–20.

DIAMOND, EDWIN, "The New Campaign Journalism," *Columbia Journalism Review,* 14, no. 6 (1976), 11–14.

———, "Would You Welcome, Please, Henry and Liv and Jackie and Erica!" *Columbia Journalism Review,* 14, no. 3 (1975), 42–46.
People-oriented journalism in magazines and newspapers.

DREW, DAN G., "Reporters' Attitudes, Expected Meetings with Source, and Journalistic Objectivity," *Journalism Quarterly,* 52, no. 2 (1975), 219–24, 271.

EFRON, EDITH, "Is There a Network News Bias?" in *Readings in Mass Communication: Concepts and Issues in the Mass Media,* 2nd ed., eds. Michael C. Emery and Ted Curtis Smythe (Dubuque, Iowa: Wm. C. Brown, 1974).

"Fulbright on the Press," *Columbia Journalism Review,* 14, no. 4 (1975), 39–45.
Sobering criticism from a veteran senator.

"Gossip Mania," *Newsweek,* 87, no. 21 (1976), 56–64.
Comment on the resurgence of gossip columns in newspapers during the 1970s.

HIRSH, MICHAEL, "The Sins of Sears Are Not News in Chicago," *Columbia Journalism Review,* 15, no. 2 (1976), 29–30.
A case illustrating advertiser influence on the newspaper press.

Hulteng, John L., "The Crux of Panax: The Performance or the Power?" *The Quill,* 65, no. 9 (October 1977), 23–25, 29.
A clash over ethics between a chain owner and two of his editors.

JANOWITZ, MORRIS, "Professional Models in Journalism: The Gatekeeper and the Advocate," *Journalism Quarterly,* 52, no. 4 (1975), 618–26, 662.

JOHNSTONE, JOHN W. C., "Organizational Constraints on Newswork," *Journalism Quarterly,* 53, no. 1 (1976), 5–13.

KURALT, CHARLES, "Journalism Is Crisis-Ridden; The Country Is Not," *Bulletin of the American Society of Newspaper Editors,* no. 592 (1976), 13–15.

"The New Ballyhoo!!!" *Columbia Journalism Review,* 15, no. 3 (1976), 39–44.
Is it neosensationalism, or just personalizing the news?

"The New Look of TV News," *Newsweek,* 88, no. 15 (1976), 68–81.

ROBINSON, JOHN P., "The Press as King Maker: What Surveys from Last Five Campaigns Show," *Journalism Quarterly,* 51, no. 4 (1974), 587–94, 606.

STERN, LAURENCE, "The Daniel Schorr Affair," *Columbia Journalism Review,* 15, no. 1 (1976), 20–26.
A case involving ethics in television journalism.

"What E. B. White Told Xerox," *Columbia Journalism Review,* 15, no. 3 (1976), 52–54.
How a respected journalist discouraged a corporation from "sponsoring" magazine articles.

Index

163